Word and Sacrament

A Preface
to Preaching
and Worship

Word and Sacrament

A Preface
to Preaching
and Worship

Donald Macleod
Princeton Theological Seminary

1960

PRENTICE-HALL, INC.

Englewood Cliffs, N.J.

This book is dedicated
to
that little company of Highland folk
who gathered Sunday after Sunday
in a simple act of worship
in the village of Broughton, Nova Scotia,
from whom I learned the accents of the Christian faith
and for whom memory holds an ever open door.

Contents

Introduction

This volume makes no other claim than its title suggests: it is a *preface*. After ten years as a teacher of preaching and worship in a Reformed seminary I have become increasingly aware of a peculiar disposition any instructor encounters among students in these related fields. In the Reformed tradition preaching and worship belong together; indeed the *raison d'être* of the former can not be fully understood apart from its context within the latter. Yet each new generation of students enters the theological seminary with at least two preconceived and faulty notions regarding the relationship of these disciplines. One group is excited over the contemporary liturgical revival and is engaged, quite unconsciously I imagine, in "the slow murder of the sermon." The other group, largely conservative in taste and theology or Puritan in emphasis, sees worship as no more than "preliminaries" and preaching as the foremost consideration.

Neither of these is insincere, but certainly each is less than half right. In their own way these groups perpetuate a stubborn remnant of that ancient dichotomy which the Reformers sought to remove, namely, the separation between Word and Sacrament. It was John Calvin's avowed intention, for example, to restore "the original liturgical unity of Christian worship," because he regarded the cleavage between Word and Sacra-

ment as "a vicious practice." In a truly meaningful act of
worship, Word and Sacrament must be correlated. If either
is emphasized to the exclusion of the other, the result will be
a truncated experience of Christian worship. This, moreover,
has serious implications for preaching because its context is the
corporate act of worship and the quality of the latter is dependent upon the integrity of the Word declared. In Reformed worship the saving Christ is proclaimed through the
Word, both preached and acted visibly in the Sacraments,
and the congregation—the community of God's people—in
response offers itself to him in adoration and in service to his
Kingdom. Hence the genius of the Protestant religion is seen
when all life becomes in essence a prolonged act of worship.

Briefly this is the burden of this book. Its chapters are
offered as a guide especially for students and young ministers
who are breaking new ground in these kindred fields. Laymen
will find historical perspective and practical suggestions here
that will assist them in their attempt to become oriented to
the revival of interest in worship and to remove much of the
confusion that exists in Reformed circles. There may be some
help here for older ministers also, who are interested in articulating the historical and theological relationship between
the two main responsibilities of their calling.

The Table of Contents indicates that the outline of this
volume falls into three discussions. Part I opens up some of
the problems that confront the contemporary preacher and
suggests how through selected emphases and a more clearly
delineated context the ministry of preaching can be reinforced.
Part II is largely historical and is an attempt to put the fruits
of the development of the Reformed liturgical tradition in
their right perspective. Part III shows how preaching comes
into its own within the context of an act of worship and suggests how that act is best formulated. The final section consists
of a number of meditations and sermons which indicate the
way the theme of worship may be presented in an informative
manner to the congregation.

It should be noted at this point that the word "Reformers" in these chapters refers to the men who championed the Reformation: Luther, Calvin, Zwingli, Bucer, Farel, Knox, *et al.* The "Reformed Churches," however, include those identified particularly with the teachings of Calvin and the Genevan heritage of liturgy and polity. Whenever it is necessary to indicate specifically those churches which were the product of English Puritanism and were Calvinistic in theology while remaining independent in liturgy, the term "Free Churches" is used.

I wish to express my appreciation to the American Association of Theological Schools for a generous Fellowship which permitted me to pursue reading and research in England and Scotland during the academic year 1958–59. To the Librarians of Trinity College, Glasgow; New College, Edinburgh; the British Museum, Dr. Williams's Collection, and Sion College, London, I owe a debt of gratitude for their courtesy in extending privileges to me and their assistance in searching out authors and titles. To Mrs. Emma A. Rowles a word of thanks is in order, for her careful typing of the manuscript for publication.

Donald Macleod
Princeton Theological Seminary
Princeton, New Jersey

Word and Sacrament

*A Preface
to Preaching
and Worship*

PART I

Preaching

1

The Integrity of
Preaching

The only justification for writing a book of this type is that in every decade the problems of preaching must be taken up and discussed anew. Indeed there is an inevitability about this periodic diagnosis, because the Protestant Church by its very nature and genius engages constantly in two simultaneous operations: re-examining itself in the light of Holy Scripture and measuring its health by its impact upon the *mores* of the times. And since preaching is one of the Church's most distinctive acts, the second part of this process of evaluation can not fail to include it. It is more than a clever aphorism to say that as goes preaching, so goes the Church.

This would indicate therefore that preaching can never take place in isolation. Indeed, its deepest significance is realized only within the context of meaningful acts of worship which comprise the Church's primary business. Here preaching can never be less than an integral and determinative factor.

Herbert H. Farmer has defined very properly the place of preaching in the Reformed tradition when he wrote, "To make and deliver sermons is a specialized function within the total life, the work, witness, and worship of the Christian community as a whole."[1]

Any discussion of the nature and effectiveness of preaching during a given period runs sooner or later into some consideration of its problems. These, however, do not vary greatly from one generation to another, but whatever differences do occur among them are discovered usually to be essentially in areas of emphasis or degrees of intensity. Nevertheless, on one point we can be quite clear: that there can never be a time when the integrity of preaching is not at stake either in the minister's own sense of his calling or in the life and activity of the Church itself. This problem is basic to all others. Indeed it is better to say that it comprehends them in such a manner that were the integrity of preaching guaranteed in any generation, all its other problems would be either resolved or reduced to the marginal or peripheral.

What is meant by the *integrity* of preaching? *The Oxford Dictionary* indicates that the word "integrity" comes from the Latin *integritas,* which means "to be lacking in no element," "wholeness," or "to be honest and sound." All these apply easily, and indeed necessarily, to preaching, because preaching must contain a message which, in order to serve well the Christian cause, can never be a truncated one; it requires form which ought to have wholeness if the message is to be intelligible at all; and it must have a *raison d'être* that squares with God's overture towards man's need that is something like Paul's disclosure, "Necessity is laid upon me; woe is me if I preach not the Gospel." In other words, the integrity of preaching involves three major disciplines: what to preach, how to preach, and why preach. And each of these can be dealt with adequately only within its own proper context: what to preach in its relationship to the Christian revelation; how to preach as a specialized type of communication in general; and why preach as an authentic and essential act within the pattern of a service of Christian worship. These are vital concerns of preaching if it is to speak prophetically and uncompromisingly to the human situation in any age. And whenever one or more of these is neglected or handled incompetently, the integrity of preaching is in a bad way and is likely to suffer immeasurable damage.

How does this work out in actual situations?

Let us look, first, at a period in the history of preaching when almost every major city in the English-speaking world boasted of at least one pulpiteer whose church was designated popularly as "a preaching center." These were the men whose reputations contributed to what Edgar De Witt Jones called "the royalty of the pulpit." They were exceptional pulpit figures —mostly Victorians—who were endowed magnificently with nature's gifts of human insight and oratory. They appeared upon the horizon of their times and comet-like they dazzled great assemblies of eager listeners. Their contribution to the literature of preaching, in both sermons and homiletical theory, was extensive and their influence upon scores of individual persons was decisive and lasting.

Yet, from the fuller perspective of the years, there is one question that bothers us and presses us for an answer. Regarding this royalty of the pulpit, why has it happened that only in the exceptional case the individual church survived the passing of the great personality? In many instances such men had large and impressive followings, but few had congregations in the sense that a strong, cohesive Christian community continued with well-organized zeal and undiminished vitality after their death. Each of their sermons was a work of art and a moving deliverance, but the listeners were never free from the haunting and ominous question, What will happen after he goes?

In other words, there was among them no sense of that corporateness of worship that alone can weld the Christian community together and guarantee for the Church the continuity to survive periodic changes in pulpit personalities. In these situations the preaching had substance and form to an unparalleled degree, but its integrity was impugned by the fact that no one saw it as an activity within the worship of a Christian community whose aim was "to glorify God and enjoy him forever." The "sermon tasters" were not taught that the idea of any church being merely "a preaching center" was an anachronism in the Reformed tradition and that inevitably this notion must be faced with the question: Why preach? And no answer is more lamentably inadequate than that preaching is done simply to provide a talented individual with an unrivalled opportunity to perform or express himself. Preaching, if its integrity is to be maintained, must have a context, and, as we shall see more clearly later, only a congregation, worshipping as Christ's Body, can provide or guarantee it. As P. T. Forsyth has cautioned us, "His [Christ's] Church is not the arena for his [the preacher's] individualism, much less his vanity."[2] True preaching presupposes, therefore, not an audience, but a Church which the preacher has built up as a compact Christian community. Only then can preaching go to the world with an authentic proclamation. May it not be that the neglect of this further aspect of the integrity of preaching can account for the lack of strong continuity in the life and witness of many individual Reformed churches?

The second situation arises, not from a sense of failure, but, curiously enough, in the midst of the Church's apparent success. Today we find ourselves midway through the twentieth century during which the fortunes of the Church have ebbed and flowed from comfortable neutrality to daring adventure and expansion. In America, for example, it has become rather commonplace to say that since World War II we have experienced a religious heyday, to such a degree that most of us have ceased to wonder at rising statistics and constantly expanding plans and programs. Any set of comparative figures shows distinctive gains in church membership, safe financial balances, and more than casual interest in what religious leaders are saying and thinking. Consequently, there has grown up a disposition among church folk to greet these indices with an air of self-satisfaction and to take them in their stride.

There is, however, a curious angle to all this, and indeed in many ways a disturbing one: this expansion has not been due in a clearly definable sense to *preaching,* except in some isolated cases. This burgeoning interest in religion in contemporary American suburbia is traceable sometimes more easily to "me-too-ism" and "the socially acceptable thing to do" than to the drawing power of the preacher's Sunday morning sermon. There seems to be "something in the wind," whether it be community pressure or the desire for social recognition or an apprehensiveness over the persistent international debacle (which is never lasting), that wields a stronger influence than the exactness of the preacher's exegesis or the orthodoxy of the doctrines he presents.

Certainly no preacher can remain happy or at ease in the face of this situation, especially when he considers the implications that lie beneath the surface. Moreover it leads him to ask questions which can bring only uncomfortable answers. He cannot, for example, avoid the query: How goes it with preaching? And for the answer he need not go any further than to examine certain facts that are writ large across the face of every parish. People are attending worship in very sizeable numbers, yet religious illiteracy is widespread and is increasing at an alarming rate. It is true that less than a fraction of those who sing with apparent abandon

> O, use me, Lord, use even me
> Just as Thou wilt, and when, and where . . .

ever realize that thereby they have committed themselves to live by Christian precepts during the week and that real worship will inevitably have social expression as one of its byproducts. Indeed more than one preacher has felt a chill of futility when a parishioner remarks in the vestibule, "Yes, what you say may be very true, but do you really expect us to live up to it?"

Again the integrity of preaching is at stake, and the preacher himself is sent back to his study to search his own soul and to grapple with further questions: Why is preaching not making the impact it ought upon this twentieth century society? Why is it not molding or giving some meaningful direction to this revival of interest in religion and thereby equipping people with a new and meaningful conception of the Church? Is the efficacy of modern preaching of so little consequence that most of us agree with John A. Mackay when he said, "The forces that are molding the opinions of youth in America today are not the churches, nor the universities, nor the schools, but secular powers that portend no good"? These questions indicate that the preacher of today is up against the biggest problem ever, not the haunting spectre of empty pews, but of sanctuaries full of people whose day to day attitudes are being shaped by forces which seem to be stronger than preaching and which preaching does not ordinarily touch.

Edwin C. Dargan, in the Introduction to *A History of Preaching*, wrote, "Preaching has profoundly and for the most part wholesomely influenced the morals and customs of mankind."[3] Then in a review of the preaching of the centuries he presented a thousand pages of evidence to support his thesis. Is the present time then to be an exception? G. C. Matthews call this "a golden opportunity for preaching."[4] Why is contemporary preaching apparently missing its chance? In the confrontation of these great congregations, has the voice from the pulpit really been unequal to the hour?

It is not easy to praise or blame within the limited perspective of the present and to come up with constructive suggestion or adequate safeguards. If many preachers in the past erred by neglecting or failing to create congregations whose solidarity survived the removal of "the pulpit star," the modern Reformed preacher must face up to his own immediate problem—the integrity of preaching in an era of religious renaissance and revival. In these times that are marked by fuzzy conceptions of what the Gospel really is and by extraordinary secular efforts to capture people's interest, he must take pains to articulate his message, to improve the form of its communication, and to re-think its place within the liturgical tradition of his own denomination. Only preaching that declares the whole Gospel of the New Testament with telling impact upon a company of persons united in an act of common worship can nourish and sustain the Church at a constant degree of vitality.

In the light of the modern situation, let us examine now these three areas where the integrity of preaching is involved, in order to understand more clearly the various contingent problems and to be able to indicate more helpfully in later chapters what their solution entails.

WHAT TO PREACH

There is a sense in which the integrity of much of our modern preaching has been weakened by a frantic effort on the part of the pulpit to deliver a message that is popular. By "popular" we do not mean the sermon with "a catchy topic" or the presence of "the glamor boy" in the pulpit, but rather the message that says to people what they want to hear and that keeps them coming back for this reason only. It is so easy for the preacher to get by with some shallow moralizing and fail thereby to uncover basic human needs and prescribe painful methods of treatment. What do people generally want to hear?

Almost invariably they clamor to be given some neat and succinct formula, some simple technique, that can always be counted upon to produce an answer to what they consider to be their best desires. Among these is the desire for authority, but always of a special type. It is not an authority with a demand, but one in which they can rest comfortably; an authority that does things for them without bringing the *status quo* into jeopardy. There is also the desire to be in with the crowd, not for the sake of being its higher conscience, but to have its shelter. As for salvation—well, it must be by a quick decision with a touch of glamor here and there, with guilt disposed of almost by fiat, and certainly without the need for lonely hours in which the soul, shaken by tears, stands before its Maker, stripped of all its twentieth century advantages and comforts. Preaching which fails to disturb this frame of mind and its fictitious wants will undoubtedly be popular, but will do little to restore or maintain its own or the Church's basic integrity. Sooner or later the preacher is driven by sheer inner frustration to ask, What should I preach? Or, what is equally serious, he may experience an encounter with his own sense of motivation and with the inevitable question, What am I here for?

How to Preach

Much contemporary preaching has failed to be effective on account of the breakdown in communication between pulpit and pew. Many preachers talk to their people without ever getting on "their wave length," to use Halford Luccock's phrase. Now, to start with, this barrier is basically a matter of the lack of a common language, because the words the preacher uses are frequently meaningless to his secular-minded generation. Words, such as "grace," "eternal life," "justification," or "reconciliation," leave them cold. Equally frustrating is the fact that the preacher possesses an entirely different set of concepts and presuppositions from his gadget-minded parishioners. They start off from premises that are not held in the theological world at all. What "fair play," for example, means to the preacher has overtones of the absolute, whereas for the man in the pew, it is merely a relative matter, and therefore the idea of morality having cosmic dimensions and sanctions is sheer fiction. What is more, the preacher is confronted with another fearful hurdle—the absence among his people of even a rudimentary knowledge of the Bible. Three years in seminary and many hours of subsequent study and exegesis have put him on an entirely different level from John Smith who is not quite sure whether Jude is in the Old or New Testament or whether Dan and Beersheba were not husband and wife, without even mentioning his bewilderment by a discussion of the Q document.

And further, the problem of communication in preaching has been increased by ministers who fail to see that there is a marked difference between communication as a secular matter and communication in preaching. There are peculiar qualities, attitudes, and presuppositions involved in preaching as communication which some speech technicians fail to see. And it has been therefore the fault of too many preachers to ape the techniques of the television expert, useful as these may be, and to feel that by these methods alone they can do full justice to their preparation to proclaim the hidden mysteries of the Gospel. But the difference between a television audience and a Christian congregation prevents a speaker from adopting in full the repertoire of the technical expert. People enter the church as individuals, but very soon they become a group, sharing a common experience at the same time in the same place. They and the preacher become together a real and tangible part of the worship experience. But the television speaker addresses himself maybe to one person or one family —some of whom dare him to interest them—whose reactions and emotions can not be shared either by the speaker himself or by the other millions who are watching at the same time.

There is a sense also in which much contemporary preaching has failed to grip its hearers because it is emotionally impoverished. Now there is an obvious difference between preaching with emotion and emotional preaching. Sheer emotionalism that is an end in itself or that is associated with whipping up a sticky form of piety has done much to discredit preaching, especially in the eyes of intelligent people. But equally ineffective has been preaching that lacked emotion entirely. "No converted man," writes Douglas Webster, "can preach Christ Crucified without some emotion, however controlled."[5] Recently someone asked the Moderator of the United Church of Canada what he thought of the preaching he heard across the country and he replied that much of it was competent but "not very inspiring." And W. B. J. Martin, in his book *Five Minutes to Twelve,* writes, "The sermon in the typical Protestant Church is an argument to be followed, whereas it ought to be an event to be experienced."[6] The affirmation of the great Christian certainties from the lips of men who have lived by them, and who therefore endorse them with flaming conviction, would tend to counteract the failure of preaching to maintain its integrity in a confused and distraught age. Helen Gardner, writing of the art of T. S. Eliot, has a word for the preacher too: "It is not the poet's business to make us believe *what* he believes, but to make us believe *that he believes.* He must convince us that he is himself convinced."[7]

WHY PREACH

Preaching in the Reformed tradition can never be rightly apprehended apart from its relationship to an act of worship. To quote Forsyth again, "The Protestant idea is that preaching is part of the cultus. To regard it as an adjunct is Roman Catholic. To regard it as a mere exposition of the minister's views is neither Protestant nor Catholic. It is not even Christian."[8] Unfortunately, in many churches this relationship between preaching and worship is only vaguely understood and by most ministers poorly defined, and hence the integrity of preaching is invariably in jeopardy. The tendency is to divorce preaching from worship, or to emphasize one at the expense of the other, which is to weaken both of them. Again the integrity of preaching has to be insisted upon and some necessary safeguards reiterated and applied. This can be done only through the recognition of three facts:

Preaching is indispensable to worship

Worship, to put it simply, is the Church's response to what God has done for men in Jesus Christ. As Raymond Abba has put it, "Worship depends upon revelation, and Christian worship depends upon the revelation of God in Jesus Christ."[9] It is man's overture of faith, thanksgiving, and obedience to the proclamation of the mighty act of God. As in Isaiah's experience in the Temple (Chap. 6:1–8), the vision came first, and then by reason of its authentic note, the prophet responded with the surrender of his whole being. By the same token, if the preaching that is within the context of worship is not of a quality and substance commensurate with that blazing unveiling in the Temple, any response to it may not seem worth the making. And since the complexion of worship is determined by the character of the Supreme Being to whom it is addressed, the responsibility of preaching for disclosing the truth about God is magnified. Moreover, the seriousness of the matter is realized more fully when we bear in mind that the response is a necessary part of the pattern of salvation.

It is alarming to note how the function of the preacher and the purpose of his preaching have become blurred in the thinking of not a few contemporary congregations! With the risk of being dubbed as old-fashioned, one cannot help expressing apprehension and concern over the new concept of the minister as a sort of "pastor-director" of the congregation, or a sanctified business manager of an organization which he is expected to run successfully according to the standards of the local Chamber of Commerce or Board of Trade. In this capacity it is so easy for the warrant and thrust of his preaching to become dimmed or blunted. He may not appear, therefore, as the arresting figure who has said to his own soul what he says to the souls of others. Moreover, he may not impress us if he really felt the fearful weight of responsibility for what he addresses to men. Somehow we miss here "the ambassador for Christ," who comes to us from a higher

level of life with good news for those whose daily routine is
a losing battle with secular powers that are too much for them.
Worship needs preaching, but its quality must be such as
to call forth the highest praise, thanksgiving, and self-surrender.
John Calvin in one of his *Tracts*[10] emphasizes the fact that
the quality of our preaching infuses into the hearers a sense of
confidence which gives birth to prayer, thanksgiving, and commitment to God's will. "Preaching then is a vital part of worship if through it God is heard speaking through the preacher,
and the listener is made aware of the reality of God."[11]

Worship completes preaching

No preaching is complete in itself, as we intimated earlier.
It needs the context of worship to be fully itself and to ac-
complish what it intends. Its natural habitation is the Christian
community, the Church. As Hyperius (Andreas Gerhard) put
it, "The place of the sermon is the Church." It is just here,
however, that much contemporary preaching breaks down
rather badly. What is the usual mode of operations on any
Sunday morning? If it is not "Communion Sunday," the sermon
ends, a hymn is sung, and the blessing is given—then bedlam
breaks out as chattering people mill about the aisles and a
holy war rages among the organ pipes. Pleasantries are exchanged about the sermon, or particularly about some humor-
ous aside in it, and general satisfaction is felt over the fact
that "our preacher is a young man on the way up." What a
lamentable outcome of preaching! What travesty of worship! Calvin never ceased to emphasize that "it is the Church
that worships, and we worship as members of it. The congregation assembles to hear God's Word and to glorify Him, and
it is as belonging to that community that we participate."[12]
If the seriousness of this act is so lightly treated by so-called
congregations, how can the integrity of preaching be safe-
guarded or protected?

Indeed it is here also that so much of contemporary mass
evangelism fails. The "Come to Christ" routine falls short of

its best intentions unless it is a call to Christ's Church. To respond merely to a particular set of theological shibboleths can be merely an individual excursion upon the dead sea of pietism. This is how spiritual isolationists are made, but it is also how individual churches can be killed. When, however, the response to preaching is made within the context of an act of worship, the natural togetherness of preaching and worship is reinforced and their complementary character demonstrated. This response is from a community of Christians which maintains the continuity of the Church and assures its influence upon the social strata of the times.

Preaching itself is worship

The integrity of preaching is secure whenever it is itself an act of worship. This is conditioned, however, by the integrity of the preacher himself. The minister's primary job is preaching and for that purpose he is a Servant of the Word to—and not for—the Church. If he is sincere, it will be to preaching that he will give his life. As Forsyth described it, "His [God's] Word engrosses his life."[13] And as he faces his congregation Sunday after Sunday, he will address that Word to them, but there will be a sense in which he presents it also to God as his own offering. The sermon is the product of his whole being because his life and experience have been poured into it. Chrysostom once said, "My whole priesthood is to teach and preach the Gospel. This is my oblation. This is my sacrifice." With the early Apostles also, preaching was "an essential part of their grateful, worshipful response to the Word of Grace which had found them."[14]

In view of these high conceptions of preaching, and with the integrity of modern preaching always in the balance, can we afford to permit it to be anything less?

2

Preaching as Communication

Ecclesiastical sensitivity to success or failure in the field of communication has recently been increased, and indeed aggravated, by the rapid invasion of the instruments of mass media into every area of our common life. It is not surprising, therefore, that questions are being raised in church circles about the apparent neglect by many preachers of some of the rudimentary requirements of good communication. For, after all, in the barest sense, preaching is the transferring of something from one mind to another, although as we shall see later, in preaching the nature of the matter communicated (what to preach) and the end result that is sought (why preach) are very different from the aims and purpose of a secular speech or declamation. In many definite ways, preaching, to quote Frederick W. Schroeder, "seems to be the noblest form of communication known to man."[1] Yet it is basically a human act of communication and therefore the preacher must never overlook the fact that there is a man at both ends of the sermon: the man in the pulpit and the man in the pew. He must examine and appropriate whenever useful the standards and methods of good communication and show greater concern for them than many contemporary preachers are inclined to give.

LITERARY REQUISITES

Communication in preaching is a matter of language, although the witness of the pulpit is not and can not ever be simply a matter of semantics. It is true nevertheless that "without speech, Christianity cannot be caught."[2] Thus choice of words is involved, and what the preacher does with them in framing his own patterns of thought and in fashioning the thrust of his own concepts. John Henry Jowett, who was himself an eager student of words, deplored in his Yale Lectures the carelessness of the preacher who was "a bondslave to much-worn phraseology," and he urged him to discover "the amazing power in the newness of carefully chosen expressions, offered as new vehicles of old truth."[3] Every student, moreover, of the history of preaching realizes that the sermons, meditations, and prayers which have been preserved and cherished through the ages and which have become the common heritage of all branches of the Reformed tradition, have featured words that were fresh and timely, had patterns of thought that were carefully etched, and were fashioned by minds throbbing with spiritual vitality.

In view of the way in which these characteristics have made the preaching of some men so effective, the modern preacher comes up with the natural and inevitable questions: What can I do to make my language better suited to fulfill the aims of my preaching? How can I break out of the rigidly set patterns of easy platitudes and trite, "parsonic" phraseology?

The initial step for the preacher is to examine his own style in the light of one that is acknowledged generally as being exceedingly good. He may select the sermons of two or three

masters of literary style and set them beside the type of thing
that ordinarily he does. For vocabulary he should read several
sermons by Arthur John Gossip and note, for example, these
three kinds of writing: one, descriptive; another, the retelling
of a Biblical incident; and another, a part of a theological
discussion.

That tired, apathetic, beaten feeling that steals over us at times,
that faithless conclusion that there is no use trying further, that
things are far too dour and crabbed ever to be straightened out, but
must remain much as they are, is foreign to Christ. We allow ourselves to be tamed by life, grow broken, unexpectant, disillusion-
ized, drift with the times as being the only thing that we can do.
But He feels that in the same world with God anything may happen; and He will set no limit to what that may be. . . . Boldly He
goes to the most hopeless-looking and impossible people and
startles them out of themselves into a better life by the sheer daring
of His hopes for them, and the glory of His faith in them, and the
audacity of His unquestioning belief in the hugeness of what He is
quite sure they are prepared to give and do.[4]

In the porches of Bethesda, He [Christ] once came on a poor
soul who had had a bleak and wintry life of it. Will you accept your
health, He asked, will you take it if I offer it to you? That sounds
cruel. Yet it was not cruel. There was an eagerness upon Christ's
face, an odd thrill in His voice. Here at last, He felt, was one for
whom He could do something. For have you ever thought out
why in all that sorry little crowd of miserable, broken things He
healed no more than one? Apparently the rest had grown dulled,
listless, apathetic, half content. After all, they were spared the heat
and dust and toil of others; and, once you got accustomed to it,
it was no bad life to lie there in the cool of the shadows, watching
the shimmering of the water, and with the pleasant sound of an
occasional copper tinkling into one's can. But here at last was one
with his face all a lean wistfulness, and his heart an obstinate ache
for what still never came. And our Lord's eyes grew bright. Will
you accept it?—and it was He who was the more eager of the two—
here, take it; and already He was heaping it upon him with both
busy hands.[5]

Stand by the Cross, and surely you must see that what God means
by loving is an amazement we can never understand, a thing that

has no ends nor bounds nor limits anywhere. What it can do, or can not do, I do not know. But after my experience of it, anything seems possible. All that is sure is that we, one and all, even the worst of us—yes, this whole blundering earth of ours—are hemmed in and surrounded by this unthinkably glorious thing, so strong, so patient, so enduring, so not to be shaken off, that however desperately we have failed Him, that however often we have thwarted Him, that however far we may have wandered from Him, God still loves us; and that there is no place in all His universe where that love of His is but a faded memory of what once was but is not any more; that even though men make their beds in hell, God, who is love, and cannot cease from loving, loves them even there.[6]

In these quotations, he will note for example the following phrases: "beaten feeling"; "faithless conclusion"; "grow broken"; "the hugeness of what He is"; "bleak and wintry life of it"; "the cool of the shadows"; "this whole blundering earth of ours." Is it likely that the pedestrian preacher would ever have selected such words? Or, in the first place, would he have accepted the semantic drudgery involved in seeking them out and incorporating them into the fabric of his style? And what is more, because he refuses to accept the necessity of being a student of words, do the right ones ever arise spontaneously from his sub-conscious at the critical moment? As R. E. C. Browne has put it, "Much labor is the antecedent of all spontaneity in writing."[7] Someone said about Joseph Parker's vocabulary that "each one was the inevitable word for his purpose." Only a full vocabulary can be an adequate vehicle for all the subtle nuances of modern thought. If therefore a preacher becomes aware of his need and sets out to be a conscientious student of new words, he can not do better than read widely among English and American classic writings whose authors were architects of great thoughts and phrases, and especially those books that keep the edges of his intellect sharply honed. He will discover the middle passage between what George Meredith called "rabble vocabulary" and what Jowett described as "frigid diction." These are the extremes

he must avoid. The middle passage is similar to the best description of Charles H. Spurgeon's style, "He was conversational,
but never colloquial." Almost any preacher with a discerning
eye and a sensitive ear can enhance, if not magnify, his effectiveness if he seeks to know and speak the idiom of his day;
to dramatize concretely those abstract theological concepts
that appear so meaningful to him; to incarnate in real persons
the moral and spiritual principles he advocates; and never to
lose sight of the need for showing the relevance between what
ought to be and what is.

Now the choice of words or the building up of a vocabulary
is merely preliminary to another equally essential step, namely,
the shaping of images and the molding of concepts. These tax
the preacher's vocabulary to the utmost and put his mental
acumen to the test. Here he must show himself as a student
of life, as an acute observer of the natural environment, able
to capture the complexion of things as they are. For example,
let us take a few excerpts from the sermons of Frederick Bruce
Speakman and note his extraordinary power to create vivid
images and to maintain novelty of expression. He mints these
phrases with a cleverness that is true art because it does not
call attention to itself.

Watch so many of the tears of the hour, bitter and maudlin and
unrelieved. It is all because there is a dry and rasping sob at the
heart of all modern doubts in spite of its blasé bluff.[8]

We have the ineradicable footprints of a man who walked all
over the pagan world to honeycomb it with the Christian Church,
then sat in Nero's cellar in chains and conquered Rome by writing
letters. And whenever the Church across the years has thought it
was establishing new beachheads of Christian truth, we have found
Paul's initials carved on some tree. He was there before us.[9]

He [the prodigal] trudged hesitatingly, no longer with that spring
of step and square set of shoulder and defiant tilt of head the town
had known and laughed about and yet had loved. None of that
was left in him now. It made you wonder what he really had been
through. Yet his father had known him, had plunged down the hill
to meet him. He hadn't waited for a syllable of apology or explana-

tion, but had seized him hungrily there in the road as they clung to each other in that wordless fierceness which is the only embrace strong men seem to know how to share.[10]

Even from these few sentences, considered out of context, we can sense the advantages of fresh words arranged in homely images or the etching of new pictures against old backgrounds. These provide hooks to arrest attention and to catch vagrant minds about to lapse into wool-gathering. They assist in meeting one of the sharpest tests of all preaching which is to keep in touch with the audience. Let the preacher who is anxious to exercise his art meaningfully examine also the writing styles of both George A. Buttrick and Paul E. Scherer, who stand among the great preachers of this generation, and see how their word patterns produce a sort of contagious excitement, marked by directness, force, and imagination that give the audience a reason for listening to them and—fortunately so— for remembering what they have said.

Further it should be added that good vocabulary and arresting imagery produce and indeed guarantee that *sine qua non* of all pulpit writing: interest. Once W. M. MacGregor classified sermons according to three types: "Those that are dull; those that are duller; and those that are inconceivably dull." And George M. Gibson expressed his concern when he defined dullness as "the sin against the Holy Ghost in preaching." Unless the literary character of preaching is such that it captures the imagination of our age, people will continue to associate the descriptions of religion with humdrum and sluggish platitudes. Any preacher who fails to recognize the power of words and the prominent place of semantics in good communication does so at his own and the Church's peril.

MENTAL AND EMOTIONAL ENCOUNTER

The foregoing discussion indicates how choice of words and the creation of images are necessary and fundamental to any type of verbal communication and are applicable also in a basic sense to preaching. But the preacher has to develop other capacities regarding his style which are demanded by the character of his communication and by the nature of the hearers to whom he addresses himself. And only the preacher who has had a real pastoral relationship for an extended period with a community can appreciate the depth and reality of what is here involved. A word which has become common coin among the experts in pastoral counselling and which every conscientious preacher must reckon with if he is to be effective is *empathy*. What is empathy? Few have ever defined it more clearly in relation to preaching than Dr. Farmer when he wrote:

> It is the power to penetrate objectively yet feelingly (not emotionally) into the individual self-awareness of any man with whom we have to deal—yes, even if it repels or revolts us because of his meanness or wickedness or dullness—so that in some measure we get inside his skin, see the world through his eyes, hear the world through his ears, participate in his feelings, think his thoughts, get a sense of him as an individual with only one life to live, one death to die, so isolated in his interior life, a man with his own memories and regrets and frustrations and disappointments, one still perhaps with hopes and dreams of other things and gnawing, unsatisfied hungers, to feel something of the "might-have-been" which is in every human life.[11]

Or, as J. C. Shairp remarked about John Henry Newman's preaching, "He laid his finger—how gently, yet how powerfully! on some inner place in the hearer's heart, and told him things about himself he had never known till then."[12]

From these descriptive definitions we see that empathy has two facets: understanding and concern. And neither of these is complete without the other. As a preacher Harry Emerson Fosdick incorporated these twin factors in his sermons to a degree unmatched by most men of this generation. Indeed once he referred to his method in preaching as "counselling on a grand scale."[13] And his expressed aim always "to talk sense" in the pulpit and "to get something done on Sunday morning" indicates the measure and reality of his concern.

Whenever understanding and concern are genuinely rooted

in a preacher's own character they become part of the driving power of his spiritual calling. If these are absent, or present in merely a superficial sense, he is apt to become a professional whose aloofness from common human need is reflected in a sermon that resembles an essay. Such a preacher was well described by Joseph Dawson as "a man in whom acquirement is at a maximum and human nature at the minimum."[14] This brings us back again to the matter of vocabulary, although in this immediate connection it is a matter of grammatical syntax, and it involves even the use of personal pronouns. A preacher should not use the impersonal pronoun "one" at all, except in making difficult distinctions in agency. He should use "me" infrequently, and "I" and "you" more frequently. Bishop Villers once said that "we" is a word for kings, editors, and corporations to use, and they alone, and that parish clergymen should always talk of "I" and "you." Indeed "I" and "you" have always been in the New Testament the great words of Good News to men. Dr. Farmer called them "the points of focus,"[15] where the preacher seeks to draw his message together and to drive home its challenge or appeal. Included here also should be what we may call "intimacy signals"[16] (e.g. "as you remember," "we have seen thus far," or, "as experience has taught us"), which the preacher can use to identify his mind and that of his hearers with similar events, feelings, and problems.

While the expression of this understanding and concern is made through the directness that suitable grammar and composition provide, yet the realization of its fuller dimensions and implications is possible only through the deeper encounter the preacher makes with his people. At this point he must satisfy his people, and he will know whether or not he is doing so by the satisfaction he himself receives from his spiritual investment in his ministry. Indeed the highest satisfaction of any man's preaching ministry is to feel the tug of humanity upon his own heart and to see the magnificent way in which the Gospel can meet man's insufficiency. This concern becomes intensely real when the preacher develops such rapport with his people that they feel he knows their plight, that he has a word for them, and that he is actually getting under the burdens they carry. When such is the case, then his word to them need not be more than what Dr. Farmer suggests: "Here and now God's saving activity in the world in Christ once again encounters the souls of men."[17] For in every congregation there are groups of people who are complex bundles of failures and hopes, of doubts and certainties, of prejudices and passions, of greatness and pettiness, and before all of them the preacher must show himself a person of clear understanding and sensitive concern. Adam Philip once said, "One of our greatest needs as preachers is a bigger humanity."

This concern will fall somewhat short of its purpose, however, if it be not on fire. It must be sounded with an ominous accent. This does not mean that the preacher must rant about the Day of Judgment being just around the corner or that somehow he has divined the fact that we are now in the latter days, sincere as he may be in his cosmic forecasts. It means that a sense of urgency must be infused into his message. Indeed there is at present in our preaching too little of the decisive note, "Now is the time!" It is, however, less of an idea than a mood, and to be sincere and valid it must have certain presuppositions in the preacher's mind. It presupposes that the preacher's approach to his job has somewhat in it of what Denney meant when he said: "Preaching is faith's testimony to Christ, to what he is and has done." If the Good News of the New Testament has meant something real and revolutionary to the preacher himself, his presentations to his people will have that "blood-earnestness" which one of his friends found so facinating in Thomas Chalmers. Recently an American news commentator laid the emphasis in the right place when he spoke on "The Responsibilities of Television," and reminded the fellow members of the panel that a speaker is remembered if (i) he knew what he was talking about, (ii) had fire in his belly, and (iii) was able to communicate.[18]

MORAL NECESSITIES

Earlier we stated that communication in preaching implies more than it does in an ordinary secular address or essay. Effective communication in preaching has always involved the preacher's moral character. Paul was conscious of this pitfall when he expressed his fear lest, having preached to others, "I myself should be a castaway." To be more specific, the quality that needs to be restored to the preaching ministry today is honesty. Now, whenever we consider honesty in preaching we think of right scriptural interpretation, absence of plagiarism, fair acknowledgment of illustrations, and refusal to pontificate beyond the range of one's own spiritual experience. Here the very obvious—and indeed some of the greater—sins of the clerical flesh are intimated, and scores of homiletical books have discussed them more adequately than need be done here. But there is the matter of dishonesty in areas and places where unfortunately its presence is overlooked and its significance regarded as trivial. Buffon once said, "Style is the man himself." How few preachers stop to realize that *how* they write is a reflection of their moral character. Ezra Pound said, "Every literary sin fritters away a scrap of your own sincerity."[19] Slovenly writing of sermons and prayers is the reflection of slovenliness within. Thinking one thing and, by clumsy expression, meaning something else is misrepresentation and is immoral. The student who says that he doesn't care about his writing style because his sermons will never appear in print is not only wholly lacking in right ambition, but he is a traitor to the literary gifts his Creator gave him. And what is more, he is on the way to becoming the victim of a slow corruption that wants to get by with as little effort as possible and is prone always to lay on God's altar an offering which has cost him very little.

Then there is the matter of honesty in the preacher's basic aim. If communication in preaching is unlike the latest telecast, here is the actual difference. Technically there are many parallels, but for the preacher the main difference is purpose. An essay or scientific lecture is framed to inform and may consist of a collation of historical or technical facts which can be either noted or rejected with impunity on the part of the speaker and hearer. But the preacher has a peculiar aim in communication. The French used to speak of *la prédiction de conquête*, by which they indicated that preaching was intended not merely for the purpose of giving good advice or to sow seeds that might some day bear fruit in a generation by better moral character. They felt it was the job of the preacher to be *out to conquer*, to take men captive for Christ, and to draw them to the foot of the Cross for pardon and deliverance. And all great preaching has done this by awakening human emotions, by effecting the deeper recesses of conscience, and by pointing the aspirations of men to higher spiritual experience. Unless, however, the Gospel has done this already in the preacher's own heart he will not be honest in urging his people to acquire what he himself has not felt it to be indispensable to possess.

That leads naturally to this final word. The proof of the preacher's honesty is detected in his sense of conviction. Earnestness and conviction go hand in hand, and inevitably they show. *The Saturday Review* said once about Edward Irving, "He lived his sermons and he preached his life."[20] In other words, his convictions embraced the whole of his preaching and his life. This is the key to persuasive power also. In ordinary speaking, communication can be simply the transfer of thought, but in preaching the medium is not merely words, but the whole man is involved.

To sum up, then, preaching as communication demands clearness of statement that can be understood by all; directness and vitality that evoke response; movement and warmth that sustain interest and win people to a desired point of view; and, above all, simplicity that never fails to make the Gospel plain or understandable through the idiom of the times. But always there is a "something more" that must be emphasized, and indeed underscored. James Buchanan who succeeded Thomas Chalmers at New College maintained that the latter's pulpit power "lay far more in his deep convictions and heartfelt experience as a converted Christian than in his natural gifts as a man of genius."[21]

In view of the suggestions and observations made in this chapter, most of us will appreciate William Cowper's description of the ideal preacher.

> Would I describe a preacher such as Paul,
> Were he on earth, would hear, approve, and, own,
> Paul should himself direct me. I would trace
> His master-strokes, and draw from his design.
> I would express him *simple*, grave, sincere,
> In doctrine, uncorrupt, in *language plain*,
> And plain in *manner;* decent, solemn, chaste,
> And *natural in gesture;* much impressed
> Himself, as conscious of his awful charge,
> And *anxious,* mainly, that the flocks he feeds
> May feel it, too; *affectionate* in look,
> And tender in address, as well becomes
> *A messenger of grace to guilty men.*[22]

3

Preaching as Proclamation

Naturally any discussion of communication presupposes something to be communicated. In preaching this is of major consequence because *what* is communicated provides the reason for and determines the pattern of the act of communication. In the previous chapter we saw that the *how* of communication in preaching differed distinctly from other modes of secular communication, although many of these are appropriated or employed by all effective preachers. This difference is created by the fact that whereas in every spoken communication a word is given, in the case of preaching it is *the Word* that counts absolutely.

Recently a minister of another denomination asked half in jest and half from curiosity, "What do Reformed preachers mean when they talk always about preaching *the Word?*" Unknowingly he was getting at a vital point, for if the preacher is not proclaiming the Word, even the inner quality of his calling is very likely to become suspect.

Now what really is meant in the Reformed tradition when young men especially are cautioned to be sure to proclaim the Word of God? Many years ago W. M. Taylor put it this way: "You are to be ministers of the Word . . . the Bible is your text . . . the very thing you are to teach is the Word of God."[1] What was implied by this? What did Karl Barth mean by a similar remark about his own early ministry: "I wanted to speak to the people in the infinite contradiction of their life, but to speak the no less than infinite message of the Bible"?[2]

These statements suggest that although God speaks to men through various media—through nature, persons, and events—chiefly has he spoken to them through a book. That book is the Bible. It must be pointed out, however, that the Bible is not itself the revelation but is the record of God's revelation of himself, which came to its climax in the person of Jesus Christ. This is the meaning of Hebrews 1:1–4. Or, as R. H. Fuller wrote, "The Bible is the record of that revealed Word, but the Word itself is Jesus Christ."[3]

In the Biblical context, moreover, the Word never means a label or a vocal sound; it connotes *action*. This is the sense in which John used it in the Prologue to the Fourth Gospel. In referring to the advent of Jesus he chose the designation, Word, rather than some other term, because it suggested activity. "In the beginning was the Act or Deed. . . ."[4] As Dr. Fuller further suggests, "God's Word is always God's act." His greatest and most decisive Word to men, therefore, was in an act by which he came into history in the person of his Son. And that person, not the Bible itself, is the Word or Act of God. At the same time, however, it must be emphasized that the Bible can never be separated, or indeed rightly interpreted or understood, apart from Christ. As Richard Davidson put it so well, "The Bible has a center and meaning: and that center and meaning is Christ. Christ is the meaning of Scripture as a whole."[5]

At this point we see more clearly what is actually implied

in the usual injunction to ministers, "Preach the Word." The
preacher's theme must be constantly that God has spoken.
And the Bible must continue to be the chief nourisher of all
true Christian preaching. It contains the record, and in dependence upon it the preacher must proclaim what God has
done. Moreover, in keeping close to the Bible the preacher
has the best assurance and guarantee that the *what* of his
communication in preaching will be nothing less than the
amazing truth that God acted "for us men and our salvation"
in Jesus Christ.

The twentieth century preacher who adheres to this point
of view shares also the heritage of a great tradition. The
preaching of the early apostles featured primarily the *kerygma*
which, in essence, was the proclamation "that prophecy was
fulfilled; that in Jesus of Nazareth, in his words and deeds,
his life and death and resurrection, the new age had arrived;
that God had exalted him, that he would come again as Judge,
and that now was the day of salvation."[6] Curiously enough,
when they proclaimed what God had done, something happened also in the lives of those who heard them. From humble
folk to persons of influence an encounter was experienced
with the Spirit of God. It plumbed their nature to the depths
and so shattered every selfish ambition and so revolutionized
their outlook that they ceased to live for themselves and began
to live for Christ. This, moreover, in varying degrees has been
part of the character of all authentic preaching throughout
the succeeding centuries. And the record has indicated on the
other hand that whenever ministers have drawn upon themselves for the basis and substance of their preaching, their
message became merely the hollow echo of their times. But
if the accent has been upon the Word which took ultimate
form in Jesus Christ, such preaching has carried the only true
imprimatur it needs or can really have.[7]

What does all this mean to and at the same time demand
from the modern preacher? To put it simply and practicably
it means that he must use the Bible more fully and centrally

in his preaching. To achieve this, and indeed to guarantee it, he must approach the Bible with certain developed skills and with a particular frame of mind—as student, as disciplined thinker, and as devout listener.

Doubtless the contemporary pulpit has lost much popular respect through the lack of a sufficient number of Biblical students among its preachers. On the other hand, no congregation wants a preacher whose discourses are parched deserts of Hebrew syntax or the *minutiae* of Greek exegesis. Yet there is a real contemporary need for preachers who will continue systematic Biblical study beyond their senior examinations in the seminary. Addressing students in divinity years ago, Dr. Gwatkin admonished them, "Do not keep dusty Bibles!" He might well have included dictionaries, lexicons, and commentaries. They too must not be neglected while the modern preacher struggles frantically to come up with some reasonable pattern of priorities. Most American preachers, especially the middle-aged, will use a customary "escape clause"; they claim that they are caught in a ceaseless whirl of activities—domestic, civic, and congregational—from which they can not possibly extricate themselves. At the same time, none of them will gainsay the fact that the preacher can never expect his pulpit to be a joy or satisfaction, but always a frightful chore, unless he comes to it with intelligent Bible study, enlightened by the use of at least one of the original languages of Scripture, and with a harvest of seminal ideas garnered in those quiet hours that are snatched from the tyranny of social and ecclesiastical trivia.

The student must also be a thinker. This is the disciplined aftermath of the hours spent on excursions into Scripture with lexicon and commentary. For this reason and purpose no preacher should complain about a rainy morning, a slow and tedious train journey, or an unavoidable delay or stopover between flights. On such occasions which have frequently disrupted nicely-laid schedules or itineraries, some of the most fruitful thinking has been done and the finest creative

insights written down. It is almost invariably during this later
period of mental ferment, after days of seemingly fruitless
mulling over an intriguing, though baffling, passage of Scripture, that the truth has flashed in upon the soul. There seems
then to be a sort of "given-ness" to it. A sincere preacher will
invariably leap for joy when suddenly he has seen the relevance to common life of a new spiritual principle and he will
be ill at ease until he can enter his pulpit to proclaim it. Indeed this must have been how the ancient prophets felt, although to a more profound degree, when they prefaced their
spiritual disclosures with "Thus saith the Lord."

The preacher must not fail to be a devout listener also. This
is the immediate counterpart of disciplined thinking. Frederick
W. Robertson, two years before his death, remarked to a friend
about preparing to preach: "Receive—imbibe—and then your
mind will create. Poets are creators because they are recipients.
They open their hearts to Nature instead of going to her with
views of her already made and second hand; so with Scripture—
patient, quiet, long, reverent listening to it; then suggestive-
ness. In other words, make the Word a daily meditation and
the interpretation will come."[8]

Such devout waiting and listening for the Word through
Scripture requires two things in particular: (a) seriousness,
and (b) personal involvement in divine truth.

(a). The preacher must approach the Bible not in a specu-
lative fashion or mood of detachment, and certainly not with
a cavalier turn of mind. He will search the Scriptures seriously.
Learned investigation, commendable and necessary as it is,
will never of itself fully unlock Gospel truth. It is to the
obedient mind and the subdued will that the Bible discloses
its message. It is the serious prayer of faith that unlocks the
shutter so that light will flood the soul. Karl Barth understands
all this so well, for he writes, "The whole Bible authoritatively
announces that God must be all in all; and the events of the
Bible are the beginning, the glorious beginning of a new
world. . . . This is within the Bible. It is within the Bible for

us. . . . Oh, that we dared in faith to take what grace can
offer us."[9]

(b). Preaching makes a greater demand upon the minister
than any other type of communication because it requires
personal involvement in its spiritual truth. And the lack of
this has been the source of the failure of much modern preaching. Every sermon ought therefore to be a living organism.
It must contain, in order to be basically a sermon, some truth
about God and man, but this by itself will not make it preaching. It must somehow come to life. Now truth in Holy Scripture is living in that it possesses a divine potential, but it will
remain dormant until it is permitted to lay its claim upon
the preacher's own soul. He must live it before he can proclaim its saving efficacy to others. As Leslie Tizard writes,
"The true preacher seeks to do one thing, and one thing only
—so to put himself in the hands of God that God may bring
about the personal encounter through him."[10] There is a sense
in which there is no such thing as making a sermon; it is
created. And the ultimate effectiveness of this creation depends upon the extent to which the preacher's own personality
is involved in it. Phillips Brooks defined preaching as "truth
through personality." In these days this definition is criticized
by those who haggle over the point that Brooks made no
allowance for the different species of truth. But they fail to
take notice of the preposition he uses, which in all likelihood
he chose deliberately—*through.* Only spiritual truth comes
through personality in the way Brooks meant it, that is through
the personality of the preacher who has himself been transformed by God's eternal truth. "Truth through personality
is our description of real preaching. The truth must come really
through the person, not merely over his lips, not merely into
his understanding, and out through his pen. It must come
through his character, his affections, his whole intellectual
and moral being. It must come genuinely through him."[11]

It is at this point that the *how* of preaching as communication and the *what* of preaching as proclamation come together

and lead us to the further and indeed ultimate question: Why preach? This matter will be resumed later when we examine the place of preaching within the context of the act of worship in the Reformed tradition.

The discussions of the two foregoing chapters will not be entirely helpful as long as they remain as mere reflections upon the theory and techniques of preaching. Let us carry the study further and present the initial stages of the creating of the sermon.

If the preacher is to interpret the Holy Scripture to his people, he must discover what is God's Word in a particular text or passage and bring it to bear with a mood of concern upon some need or problem among his people. He must not begin with the problem, because then his preaching will lose the element of proclamation and will have a range no greater than the gamut of the human ills the preacher himself knows. He must begin with the Word and allow its white light to shine upon the common scene where it will expose our frailties and relate its redemptive power to them. It is in this act that the interpreter's genius comes to its fruition. This will the preacher ultimately offer to God and to his people within the context of the act of common worship.

In seeking a method for understanding, one of the most helpful writings is H. A. Hodges' introduction to Wilhelm Dilthey's scholarly *Gesammelte Schripten* where he states that understanding requires a threefold background of knowledge: the nature and significance of the literary work in its historical tradition; the exact meaning that its language implies; and the peculiar claim the writer's message makes upon us.[12] What is requisite here to our understanding of any literary work is applicable also to our understanding of the message and relevance of the Bible. The preacher's task is threefold: historical, exegetical, and interpretative. And these three movements spell out the *modus operandi* of all good preaching. To emphasize any one of these to the neglect of the others is to destroy that wholeness which otherwise has characterized preaching with real understanding.

Suppose the Scripture selection for the sermon is Psalm 73.

Historical: Psalm 73 is one of the eleven so-called "Asaph Psalms." It is attributed to Asaph, the Gershonite, who was one of David's chief musicians, a player on the cymbal and a song writer, hence a Psalmist. One of the most distinctive features of this group of Psalms is their prophetic character.

Exegetical: This Psalm has two two main movements: (i) The writer tells of the origin and nature of his temptation; and (ii) he describes the final conquest of doubt.[13] As Samuel Terrien put it: "In the form of a meditative prayer in two parts he recounted his peregrinations through the seas of scepticism until he reached the haven of grace."[14] In other words we have here a poignant little drama of a man's struggle with himself and a great world problem, and all within the area of one human soul. It is a vignette of Job's dilemma. Indeed it sweeps the whole circle of our common humanity. And it is peculiar in that it is never a blunt doubting of God's actual existence, but a more delicate thrust: it questions whether or not God can be relied upon as the end and focus of faith. Like so many of the Psalms, it begins with a conclusion (vs. 1)—compare also Psalms 23 and 121—and then follows the clear pattern of Asaph's inward experience: doubt (vs. 2); how it arose (vss. 3–14); some solutions of the problem (vss. 15–20); the victory of faith (vss. 21–28). The crossroads of the Psalm, however, is verse 17 and the Journey's End is verse 28: "It is good for me to draw near to God."

In order to point up the issue that is involved in this Psalm and to have an integrative principle for the purpose of unity, verses 2 and 17 may be selected as the text: "But as for me, my feet were almost gone; my steps had well nigh slipped . . . until I went into the sanctuary of God . . ." A positive topic for the sermon could be "Faith Beyond the Forms of Faith," or, "What One Man Found in Church."

Interpretative: The human situation: Geo. Johnstone Jeffrey, the well-known Scottish preacher, once said that "the spiritual life is a warfare in which faith has to fight for every inch of ground." To this we may add a postscript that among faith's perennial antagonists the greatest is human doubt. Many of these doubts, however, are mere figments of our imagination or self-created negations that common sense proves eventually to be illusory and without foundation. But every man, sooner or later, meets up with the real facts of hard circumstances and is likely to become involved in a grim struggle with doubt.

The evidence of history is that our encounter with doubt is usually more stormy during a time of spiritual lapse or decay. Indeed the weaker our grasp upon the essentials of faith the greater the chance that doubt will win the day. But what about these times? Are they an exception? These are days of revival and religious renaissance, and yet doubt is actively in the field and is claiming more casualties than we dare to acknowledge. The answer can be found, we believe, in a more precise interpretation of doubt.

Doubt is not the same thing as unbelief; they are not synonymous. Granted that there are many people today who are caught in a grave struggle with doubt; there are fewer in the mood of actual unbelief. Indeed recent polls indicate almost a unanimous belief in God. At the same time we must not lose sight of the fact that doubt and unbelief are not entirely unrelated. If doubt is unchecked, it can become unbelief. And the only thing that will stop the headlong rush towards unbelief is the power of a positive faith. Obviously the chief reason doubt is on the increase today is that the faith we have does not possess virile rootage to withstand the shaking of the world. Science is moving too far and too fast for us. Laws of operation in the area of values are ruptured by ugly forces that care little for human destiny. Evil seems to be riding the wild horses of power, and timidity is frequently the best color shown by good. We may not have gone so far as to lose our grip upon belief in the existence of God,

but more and more people are wondering whether God is
not simply indifferent to the good or whether to live right is
any longer worthwhile. Fortunately we have not reached the
unhappy mood of Aldous Huxley's character who lamented,
"And suddenly the divine presence was eclipsed. There was
no God, no Christ, nothing but fear." But certainly many are
asking reflectively Satan's question: "Does Job serve God for
nought?"

(The foregoing is the human situation to which the message
of the Psalm is to be directed.)

The Psalmist's message and lessons: He did not doubt God's
existence, but he was for a time "losing the assurance of God's
mercy and love and saving power."[15] And can we blame him?
He had taken a long look at the world around him and the
tally of the facts shook his soul (vss. 3–12). He noticed that
the prosperous folk were wicked and unscrupulous men whose
material success had made them arrogant and who strode
across life's stage as if the world belonged to them. Added
to this was the galling sight of mediocre "do-gooders" who
gave homage to these coarse handlers of the earth's bounty
(vs. 10). Hence the Psalmist became envious and bitter, and
his first impulse was "to throw in the sponge" in a gesture of
futility. "Surely in vain have I cleansed my heart and washed
my hands in innocency" (vs. 13). Next a rebellious mood
seized him and he almost ran outside to howl his melancholy
tale into the ears of the world. But then he feared this would
do more damage than good (vss. 14, 15). How well has Sheldon
H. Blank paraphrased the Psalmist's experience: "Once I
envied transgressors. Sleek, smug and successful, they arro-
gantly deny God's providence. To my shame be it said, I
almost copied them. My own ascetic piety, I asked myself,
what good has it done me? But now I see I was passing through
a crisis of faith."[16]

Then the Psalmist took his difficulty into the sanctuary of
God (vs. 17a). Perhaps it was the temple. Or, better still,
it may have been some simple rendezvous where God's mys-

terious presence was especially felt. Wherever it was, the
important matter is that he chose to resort to the right place
and he gained there a new perspective, discovered himself
afresh, and began to see life and destiny within the context
of God's wisdom rather than his own (vs. 17b). The visit to
the sanctuary showed him that when a man draws "near unto
God" (vs. 28), he sees things differently. And these are as
follows:

A. *What a man is, and not what he has, is most important*
(vss. 18–29). In the presence of God, our whole system of
values is revolutionized and the objectives which ordinarily
we prized have become hindrances rather than helps. What
a man has turns to nothingness, while what he is endures.
Indeed the souls' encounter with God is the fire which has
tried every man's work (I Cor. 3:13).

B. *What a man envies is not usually the best, but the second
best* (vss. 21, 22). When the Psalmist came to his senses, so
to speak, in God's company, he was filled with painful re-
morse.[17] What he had envied in the wicked was alien to
God's nature, inimical to his own soul's welfare, and out of
keeping with the aspirations of anyone who desired and cherished goodness. He was not coveting the best, but something
far inferior. He was jealous of success that is measured in terms
of all one can grab with moral impunity and not in terms of
real meaning and values. "Covet earnestly," and Paul, "the
best gifts" (I Cor. 12:31).

C. *What a man seeks in goodness is not reward, but to be
good for goodness' sake* (vs. 28). As soon as a man puts a price
upon his devotion to the good and true, his moral deteriora-
tion and spiritual disappointment have begun. To quote Dr.
Terrien again, "Like many wise men, past and present, the
Psalmist conceived religion as a method of obtaining success
and a happy life. When the technique seemed to fail, he almost yielded to despair." James Moffatt put the matter into
proper perspective when he said, "We are not saved because
we are good. We are good because we are saved."[18]

D. *What a man is, is possible only by God's help* (vss. 23–27 and vs. 1). "Whom have I in heaven but thee?" exulted Asaph. "And there is none upon earth that I desire beside thee." God gripped him by the right hand and lifted him out of the mire of bitterness and sullen defeatism, and now he had direction because his goal was to be ever in the presence of the Most High. Now doubt was gone. And it was gone because cheap faith had been cast out. A stronger and a more costly faith had displaced it.[19]

The above study is an example of the way the proclamation of faith is set over against the agony of human doubt. The finished sermon would be a stage beyond this and would feature directness of approach, a more conversational style, more images, quotations, and illustrations. However, this example indicates how the preacher can lift out of a passage of Scripture a positive message, which is the Word of God speaking to him, and make it both the unifying factor in the sermon and the essence and thrust of the Gospel he proclaims.

For reasons of clarity, the outline of this sermon would appear as follows:

Topic: "Faith Beyond the Forms of Faith"

Text: Psalm 73: 2 and 17: "As for me, my feet were almost gone; my step had well nigh slipped. . . until I went into the sanctuary of God . . ."

I.   Introduction: Brief discussion of modern tendency to doubt:

    A. Doubt aggravated by world situation.

    B. Doubt aggravated by seeming absence of moral order.

II.   Psalmist's problem:

    A. What he saw (vss. 4–12).

    B. What it did to him:

        1. Sense of futility (vss. 13, 14).

        2. Active rebellion (vs. 15).

        3. Resignation (vs. 16).

        4. Misery is increased (vs. 16b).

III. Psalmist's strategy: Took problem to sanctuary of God (vs. 17).

IV. Result: When a man gets near God he see things differently.

> A. What a man is, and not what he has, is important (vss. 18–20).
> B. What a man envies is not usually the best but the second best (vss. 21, 22).
> C. What a man seeks in goodness is not reward, but to be good for goodness' sake (vs. 28).
> D. What a man is, is possible only with God's help (vss. 23–27 and vs. 1).

(Some of the ideas—pp. 37–40—appeared originally in an article by the author in *Interpretation*, XII, 4, pp. 418–420. Used by permission.)

PART II

Worship

4

Our Heritage in
Reformed Worship*

FROM THE EARLY CHURCH

As far as we can learn Jesus never formulated a liturgy, yet his influence upon the quality and shape of religious worship has been no less then revolutionary. This was due, doubtless, to his conviction that a man's relationship to God was the essential matter, and therefore his teaching had to do more properly with the quality of human intercourse with the Father than the prescription of a method or the setting up of forms. In reply, for example, to the disciples' request, "Lord, teach us to pray," he gave them a model,

---

* This chapter is merely a general historical survey which is included in order to avoid a lacuna in the pattern of this book. Students of church history and liturgics will find nothing very new in these pages, but it is hoped that beginners will be able to see more clearly and in better perspective the primary sources and major facets of the Reformed tradition in worship. For further reading, adequate bibliographies may be found in W. D. Maxwell: *An Outline of Christian Worship*, Oxford University Press, 1936, pp. 183–194; G. H. C. MacGregor: *Eucharistic Origins*, James Clarke, 1928, pp. 249–252; and A. Barclay: *The Protestant Doctrine of the Lord's Supper*, Jackson, Wylie, 1927.

not of the right *structure,* but of the right *kind* of prayer.

What we do find is that Jesus entered freely into the traditional worship patterns of his own people and times, although there is evidence to indicate that he was more partial to the synagogue than to the Temple. Probably the clearest and most complete account of his attending formal worship in the synagogue is found in Luke 4:16–21:

And he came to Nazareth, where he had been brought up: and, as his custom was, he went into the synagogue on the sabbath day, and stood up for to read.

And there was delivered unto him the book of the prophet Esaias. And when he had opened the book, he found the place where it was written,

The Spirit of the Lord is upon me, because he hath anointed me to preach the gospel to the poor; he hath sent me to heal the broken-hearted, to preach deliverance to the captives, and recovery of sight to the blind, to set at liberty them that are bruised,

To preach the acceptable year of the Lord.

And he closed the book, and he gave it again to the minister, and sat down. And the eyes of all them that were in the synagogue were fastened on him.

And he began to say unto them, This day is this scripture fulfilled in your ears.

And all bare him witness, and wondered at the gracious words which proceeded out of his mouth.

Other similar, though shorter, references are: Mark 1:21; 6:2. Matt. 4:23; 9:35. Luke 4:15, 16; 6:6; 13:10–17. John 6:59; 18:20. These, however, do not suggest that Jesus boycotted or disowned the Temple. It was there, at the early age of twelve years, that his parents discovered him reasoning with the learned expositors of the ancient Law (Luke 2:46). What is more, no one can prove that he did not observe or have a share in the stated festivals of the Jewish religious year which were associated traditionally with the Temple. And certainly one of the most dramatic episodes of his ministry occurred when he drove out those who in his judgment were defiling it by using its courts for commercial ends. Would he have bothered to do so or risked the consequences if in his own estimation the Temple were not truly God's House?

Apart from the example of his faithfulness to the synagogue and the Temple as the accepted institutions of his native Jewish background, Jesus' influence is known particularly by three things which he bequeathed to his disciples and which are regarded by us today as indigenous to Christian worship. These have done more than anything else to shape the worship and witness of the Church through the centuries. First, and somewhat indirectly, there was the integrity of his personal devotion to God; second, more directly, there was what he said and did during the final meal with his disciples before his crucifixion; and third, and most especially, there was the impact of his risen presence which galvanized the hopes of his followers and made them acutely conscious of their Living Lord. To these factors we are indebted for the essential character of Christian worship and when they have been recalled in faith, that is, whenever the glorified Christ has been made the focus of the liturgical act of God's people, the effect has been revolutionary.

When we read the New Testament we come upon the Christian community at worship, and although the accounts of it are very fragmentary, and sometimes contradictory, we are struck by the predominant and universal note of thanksgiving. Indeed the Greek word used in Acts 2:46 is ἀγγαλλίασις, meaning "overflowing" or "abounding joy." And F. Spitta has indicated that technically it means "eschatological joy,"[1] which suggests that it was experienced in the confidence of a final triumph of the Messianic faith. But moods are more easily sensed than forms can be delineated; yet some indication of early Christian worship can be gathered from the aggregate of the various things that were done. "And they, continuing with one accord in the temple, and breaking bread from house

to house, did eat their meat with gladness and singleness of
heart, praising God, and having favor with all the people"
(Acts 2:46, 47). "Let the word of Christ dwell in you richly;
in all wisdom teaching and admonishing one another, with
psalms and hymns and spiritual songs, singing with grace in
your hearts unto God" (Col. 3:16). "Speaking to one another
in psalms and hymns and spiritual songs, singing and making
melody with your hearts to the Lord; giving thanks always
for all things in the name of the Lord Jesus Christ to God
even the Father" (Ephes. 5:19–20). In I Timothy 3:16 we
have what may have been a fragment of an early creed. In
Ephesians 5:14, a snatch of a hymn. In II Timothy 2:11–13,
a part of an ancient liturgy. The evidence from these passages,
however vague and scanty, is sufficient to indicate that the
New Testament Church was a worshipping church,[2] and its
dominant theme was praise and thanksgiving.

At the time of Jesus, it must be remembered, the synagogue
was the center of Jewish worship and thought, while the
Temple was the symbol of their religion. Within forty years
after Jesus' death the Romans destroyed the Temple and it
was never rebuilt, but the synagogue was maintained and
continued as a house for devotion and study. Now the early
Christians, being Jews, did not break away immediately from
the synagogue, but continued for considerable time as a new
sect within Judaism.[3] It was in the synagogue, for example,
that Stephen incurred the indignation and fury of the authorities (Acts 6:9ff.). It was to the synagogues in Damascus that
Saul set out with the high priest's letters on his errand of persecution and destruction (Acts 9:2). And it was in the synagogue, after his conversion, that he proclaimed Jesus as the
Son of God (Acts 9:20). Indeed later, on several occasions,
he encouraged the observance of the traditional practices of
the synagogue: I Tim. 2:1. II Tim. 4:13. I Thess. 5:27. I Cor.
14:16. Consequently, on the sabbath, Christians would be
found in the synagogues, but on other days of the week,
chiefly the first, they engaged in the breaking of bread in

private homes (Acts 2:42; 20:7, 11. I Cor. 16:2). And when they broke finally with Judaism (circa A.D. 135), they brought the patterns of the synagogue worship with them into the new faith. As Duchesne put it, "It was the liturgy of the synagogue rather than the worship of the Temple which molded the services of the early Christian community."[4]

What then were the chief parts of synagogue worship that were familiar to the first Christians and which were to influence the services of the New Testament Church? In his scholarly volume, *The Jewish Background of the Christian Liturgy*, W. O. E. Oesterley (Chap. 2:36–82) names the following: (a) reading of the Scriptures and their interpretation; (b) recitation of the Jewish Creed, the Shema (Deut. 6:4); (c) the use of the Psalms, the Ten Commandments, the Benediction, and the Amen; (d) the Prayers; and (e) the Jewish *Kedushah*, or Prayer of Sanctification, which became in the Christian tradition the *Ter Sanctus*. All these items in some form or other found their way into the service of worship of the Christian Church.

The peculiar element, however, in New Testament worship was the new service that developed around "the breaking of bread." This phrase was not the ordinary expression for taking food, but it goes back to the Hebrew for breaking a loaf for distribution. It occurs in Luke 24:35, "and he was known to them in the breaking of bread." It is used also in the synoptics on the occasions when great numbers were fed: Mark 6:41; 8:6; Matt. 14:19; 15:36; Luke 9:16. It could be that Jesus had his own peculiar way of doing it, and in Acts the disciples may have been continuing what their Master had done when he was alive and with them. But to this custom something new had been added. As A. B. MacDonald has put it, "They gathered in private, as a company of Christian brothers, round a supper-table which, in some emphatic way, was their Master's own table."[5] The resurrection had pushed the hard fact of the crucifixion into the background temporarily and had filled the disciples with joy over Christ's spiritual presence. "The joy manifested by the early Christians during 'the breaking of bread' has its source in the consciousness they had of eating with the *Risen* Christ, really present in their midst, as he was on Easter Day."[6]

At this point, however, two questions arise which scholars have continued to explore and upon which they have failed to reach common ground. (*Cf.* H. Lietzmann: *Messe und Herrenmahl;* Y. Brilioth: *Eucharistic Faith and Practice;* G. H. C. MacGregor: *Eucharistic Origins;* M. Goguel: *L'Eucharistie des Origines à Justin Martyr.*) What was the particular meal which Jesus held with his disciples and which has come to be known traditionally as the Last Supper? How did this post-resurrection meal, with its joyful awareness of the Risen Christ, become eventually the Lord's Supper with its association and identification with the redemptive purpose of his death?

Regarding the first question, we are reminded of Dr. Denney's word of caution, "One almost despairs of saying anything about the Lord's Supper which will not seem invalid to some upon critical or more general grounds."[7] There are those who identify the Last Supper with the Passover Meal,[8] as the Synoptic writers themselves seem to do (Mark 14:12; Matt. 26:17; Luke 22:7 and 15). But the arguments against this position are too formidable to allow it to be held with much enthusiasm. A careful examination of the Synoptic accounts shows an impossible confusion in the chronology of events during those latter days, whereas John's Gospel alone presents the succession of events with a measure of plausibility, both ceremonially and historically. John's chronology rules out any possibility of the Last Supper and the Passover meal coinciding, and our knowledge of Jewish Law discounts any possibility of its being held a whole day in advance. This "Last Supper=Passover equation," to use Neville Clark's phrase, is an over-simplification. If they were identical it would mean that such events as Christ's arrest, trial, and crucifixion took place on the sacred day of the feast, which would hardly be tolerated by the Jews (Mark 14:2). And further, what is more convincing is that the form of the Last Supper differs from the pattern of the traditional Passover meal. Had it been the same thing, the paschal lamb and not bread and wine, would have been most prominent. On no occasion, moreover, does St. Paul himself regard the Last Supper as a Passover meal. J. H. Srawley's explanation of the likely source of this point of view is helpful: "The fact that Jesus suffered at the Paschal season, that he had the Passover in mind at the Supper (Luke 22:15), and that he had come to be thought of as 'our Passover' (I Cor. 5:7) would naturally lead to the conception of the solemn memorial of his death as a Christian Passover, and this influence may have affected the Synoptists' account of the actual setting of the Supper."[9]

There are some others who trace the Last Supper to the *Kiddûsh*, which W. D. Maxwell describes as a simple meal held weekly by a group of male Jews (chabûrôth), sometimes a rabbi and his followers or the members of a pious Messianic circle, in preparation for the Sabbath or another religious festival.[10] The usual meal took place, and then as the evening came, the leader would begin the Sanctification ceremony, i.e., the Passover-Kiddûsh in this case, by taking first the cup and afterwards the bread and by pronouncing over them his blessing: "Blessed art thou, O Lord our God, King Eternal, who hast chosen us from all peoples, and exalted us above all tongues, and sanctified us by thy commandments. And thou hast given us in love, O Lord our God, appointed times for gladness, festivals and seasons for joy; this day of the Feast of unleavened bread, the season of our Freedom." Despite the general similarities here and the ease with which the Last Supper could be traced to such a ceremonial, this theory can hardly be held because, as Neville Clark has reminded us, "while the Last Supper was on Thursday evening, the *Kiddûsh* took place on Friday evening. Nor was it movable; for it occurred after the feast began. It was only a day-blessing over a common cup either at the beginning or at the end of the meal. Thus the Passover would include the *Kiddûsh*, for the latter was one of the four cups at Passover."[11] And, as T. W. Manson concludes, "There is no evidence for a Passover *Kiddûsh* which takes place twenty-four hours before the feast."[12]

There is another explanation, and certainly more probable, that the Last Supper was one, and this time the most significant, of the common meals, "the breaking of bread," which had been shared between Jesus and the intimate circle of his disciples. It must be remembered that every Jewish meal had more or less a religious character; indeed none was entirely without a sacramental quality. On these occasions, Jesus as the head of the "household" blessed the bread and wine, and maybe impressed upon his disciples how symbolic were these things of their common dependence upon God for daily spiritual food. On the eve of his death, however, he conducted the meal in a grave and peculiar manner and with words that were reminiscent of a Paschal feast. Dr. Sanday explained it in this way: "If Jesus designed during the course of the meal to perform a solemn symbolical act with the bread and wine at the table . . . then it is only likely that the 'form' of this act would have a general likeness to existing religious practices at the table."[13] Or, as G. H. C. MacGregor wrote about the Supper, "It was inherited and evolved by the primitive Christian Church from current Jewish practice sanctioned and blessed by Jesus, and so transformed into a specifically Christian rite."[14] With the resurrection, "the breaking of bread" became an occasion of Christian joy and fellowship, with memories of the Last Supper with Jesus, but with a sense of victory because their Lord was *alive*.

Regarding the second question—how this eucharistic meal became the Lord's Supper with an emphasis upon Christ's death—two answers have been given, and as we shall see, the second is more or less an extension of the first. In the early chapters of Acts, Christ's death is represented as having been annulled overwhelmingly by the resurrection. In Peter's great sermon at Pentecost, he declared, "Jesus of Nazareth . . . him . . . ye have taken, and by wicked hands have crucified and slain: whom God hath raised up, having loosed the pains of death: because it was not possible that he should be holden of it" (Acts 2:22–24). But, with the passing of the initial elation over the resurrection and through subsequent reflection upon Scripture, the focus became more inclusive. Through reflection upon what the Scriptures had really said and the identification of Jesus with the Suffering Servant of Isaiah 53, his death was thrust into the picture and his redemptive work assumed therefore a new centrality. From this broadened perspective the disciples saw their Master's death as integral to God's eternal plan. It was very easy then for the fellowship meal with its thanksgiving for Christ's living presence to re-call with a similar εὐχαριστία the benefits his death had achieved for believers.

A second answer,[15] which is supported by both Alexander B. MacDonald and Oscar Cullmann, is that this union was the work of St. Paul. In so doing, however, Paul was not playing the role of an innovator or attempting to substitute some radically new idea. On the contrary, he wished to complete the eucharistic concepts of the early Church by connecting them with the Last Supper and consequently with Jesus' death. In Paul's thinking the cross and the resurrection were always closely linked; indeed for him they were twin foci of the fact of Christ. And when we examine the words of the institution of the Lord's Supper in I Corinthians 11:23–26, we realize how thorough was Paul's understanding and we see how the rite dramatized what had become his own missionary message. As Dr. Rawlinson has remarked, "St. Paul did not invent the Last Supper, but it is just possible that he was indeed the first Christian to see what it meant."

There is, first of all, Paul's own personal warrant: "For I have received of the Lord that which also I delivered unto you." The verb used for receive is παρέλαβον which implies "receiving instruction from a Christian teacher," and it occurs also in I Cor. 15:1, 3; Gal. 1:9. and Phil. 4:9. For the preposition "from," ἀπό is used which signifies "indirect reception," rather than παρά which suggests "a direct revelation." The past tense "delivered" indicates that he was not making this declaration to the Corinthian Church for the first time. He had told them before, but in view of their defaulting from true faith and practice, Paul determined to spell out matters carefully. There is the recognition of what Cullmann calls "the internal link" between the Last Supper and the eucharistic meal of the early Christians: "That the Lord Jesus the same night in which he was betrayed." There is the customary gesture, typical of every fellowship meal which Jesus shared with his disciples: "And when he hath given thanks." There is the action, the breaking of bread and the pouring of wine, accompanied by the unique designations: "This is my body, which is broken for you" and "this cup is the new testament in my blood." This is no concession, however, to transubstantiation, because "no material thing was ever to a Jew in itself a vehicle of spiritual grace."[16] There is the new covenant between Jesus and his followers, which was to be accomplished through his death. The old covenant with Israel was inaugurated through the shedding of blood; now through Christ's blood, a new covenant was formed between God and the new Israel, *the new fellowship of believers*. Finally, there is the eschatological emphasis: "Ye do show forth the Lord's death till he come." It is his death that they must remember, and as they declare it anew at each supper, it will indicate their anticipation of the final consummation of all things in the Kingdom of God.

By these words we see how "the shed blood of Christ first assumes its permanent place in the Eucharist as a result of Paul's referring back to the original source of early Christian meals, namely the Last Supper of the historic Jesus."[17] And it has been the conviction of Christians through succeeding ages that in continuing to celebrate the Lord's Supper they were acting under the guidance of Christ's spirit and were perpetuating this sacred action "in remembrance of him." There are some theologians and liturgical scholars who have maintained that Jesus never instituted this sacred rite, nor commanded it to be continued (e.g. Bernard Weiss, Hastings Rashdall, Ernest W. Barnes, Y. Brilioth, and others).

But our final decision regarding this question must depend always upon our conviction about who and what Christ was and about Christianity as a religion of redemption. And when we think upon these things we see some real wisdom in P. T. Forsyth's position when he said, "If Christ had not said 'Do this,' the Church would have been impelled to do something in response to God's greatest act."[18]

It must be noted in this instance that "to remember" did not mean to recollect a fact or to view a memorial. It had the Hebrew connotation—to remember meant to make actual a past situation. The Lord's Supper made actual for each believer what God did for man through his only Son. Moreover, for these believers, the Supper could never be merely a memorial. The resurrection was an incontrovertible fact, and therefore, "how could we have a mere memorial of one who is still alive, still our life, still present with us and acting in us?"[19] Nor must its sacrificial character ever be overlooked or interpreted in any mechanical sense, but in the way that Paul saw it within the whole context of Christian life and worship, as in Romans 12:1: "I beseech you therefore, brethren, by the mercies of God, that you present your bodies a living sacrifice, holy, acceptable unto God, which is your reasonable service."

By A.D. 65, Peter, Paul, and James were dead and the career of the early Church entered upon a new phase. The period of creative enthusiasm was over and the lines were beginning to fall into somewhat recognizable patterns. For the next seventy-five years or more, little of a concrete nature is known of the development of the worship methods of the Christian sect. During this period, however, several events occurred and

certain writings appeared which are helpful in our attempts
to reconstruct an approximate picture.

The event of greatest moment and significance was the
breaking away of the early Christian from the formal worship
of the synagogue. Eusebius[20] places it about A.D. 135, while
Dugmore[21] tends toward a gradual alienation from A.D. 90
onwards. The reasons for this break were inevitable and may
be listed as follows: (i) Tension arose over literal observance
of the written Law; (ii) Jewish antagonism to Christian belief
in a Messiah who had been put to death (the Jews wouldn't
like Rev. 5:9, 12); (iii) the inclusion in the liturgy of the synagogue around A.D. 90 of a declaration against heretics; (iv)
increase of conversions among Gentiles under Paul's missionary
influence forced the abandonment of circumcision, lest these
new Christians would feel they were being made proselytes
to Judaism; (v) with the rapid growth of the Church, Christian
worship developed to a point that made synagogue attendance
superfluous.

The second event was no less crucial, although it was a
gradual outgrowth of the first, namely, the fusion of the service
of the synagogue with the service of the Eucharist. When
this union occurred is also not clear, but Lietzmann gives us
some assistance in saying that "in the earliest period the
Eucharist belongs to the late afternoon hours. . . . By about
the middle of the second century the sacramental meal was
developed into an independent rite and has been transferred
to Sunday morning and joined with the service of reading and
preaching."[22] A. B. MacDonald agrees, when he writes, "Already by the middle of the second century, Christianity had
struck out its classic form of Sunday Service and laid down
the frame work for the worship of the future . . . which has
never been superseded."[23]

Among the writings which are our sole source of evidence
for the nature and pattern of the worship of this period, the
most suggestive are: Pliny's *Letter to Trajan*, *The Didaché*,
and Justin Martyr's *First Apology*.

Pliny's Letter to Trajan

Pliny, Roman Governor of the Province of Pontus and Bithynia, wrote to the Emperor Trajan (circa A.D. 112) and sought a clearer policy in dealing with problems created by the Christians within his area of jurisdiction. The classic paragraph ran as follows:

They were in the habit of meeting before dawn on a stated day and singing alternately a hymn to Christ as to a god, and they bound themselves by an oath, not to the commission of any wicked deed, but that they would abstain from theft and robbery and adultery, that they would not break their word, and that they would not withhold a deposit when reclaimed. This done, it was their practice, so they said, to separate, and then to meet together again for a meal. . . .[24]

The Didaché

This writing, sometimes known as "Teaching of the Apostles," is actually a manual of instruction, consisting of sixteen brief chapters and dating back to a period roughly designated by scholars as A. D. 90–110. It was unknown until discovered in Constantinople in 1875, and although its author has never been identified, internal evidence points to Syria, or even Antioch, as its geographic origin. The first six chapters consist of instructions for candidates for Baptism, and the remainder have to do with the conduct of worship, the Eucharist, and the proper treatment of various offices of the Church. Scholars have labeled this document variously and have regarded it with differing degrees of enthusiasm. W. D. Maxwell, for example, thinks it is a combination of the *Agapé* and eucharist, with some similarities with the Kiddûsh. Canon Streeter, one of the strongest supporters of its authenticity and value, wrote that "the influence of this little book on the later literature dealing with Church Order has been greater than that of any other work outside the New Testament."[25] Chapters IX and X provide prayers of εὐχαριστία and XIV gives directions for Sunday worship.[26]

IX. And concerning the Service of Thanksgiving, give ye thanks after this manner: First, concerning the Cup: We give thanks to Thee, our Father, for the Holy Vine of David Thy child, which Thou didst make known to us through Jesus Thy child; to Thee be glory for ever.

And concerning the broken Bread: We give Thee thanks, our Father, for the life and knowledge which Thou didst make known to us through Jesus Thy child. To Thee be glory for ever. As this broken bread was scattered upon the mountains, but was brought together and became one, so let Thy Church be gathered together from the ends of the earth into Thy Kingdom, for Thine is the glory and the power through Jesus Christ forever. But let none eat or drink of your Eucharist except those who have been baptized in the Lord's name. For concerning this also did the Lord say, "Give not that which is holy to the dogs."

X. But, after you are satisfied with food, thus give thanks: We give thanks, O Holy Father, for Thy Holy Name which Thou didst make to tabernacle in our hearts, and for the knowledge and faith and immortality which Thou didst make known to us through Jesus Thy child. To Thee be glory for ever. Thou, Lord Almighty, didst create all things for Thy Name's sake, and didst give food and drink to me for their enjoyment, that they might give thanks to Thee, but us hast Thou blessed with spiritual food and drink and eternal life through Thy child. Above all we give thanks to Thee for that Thou art mighty. To Thee be glory for ever. Remember, Lord, Thy Church, to deliver it from all evil and to make it perfect in Thy love, and gather it together in its holiness from the four winds to Thy kingdom which Thou hast prepared for it. For Thine is the power and the glory for ever. Let Thy grace come and let this world pass away. Hosannah to the God of David. If any man be holy let him come, and whosoever is not, let him repent. Maranatha. Amen. But suffer the prophets to hold Eucharist as they desire.

XIV. On the Lord's day of the Lord come together, break bread and hold Eucharist, after confessing your transgressions, that your offering may be pure.

Justin Martyr's First Apology

Justin Martyr was a Christian scholar and preacher who lived in Rome during the tenure of the Emperor Antoninus

Pius and his son, Marcus Aurelius, about A.D. 150. Realizing
how gravely the Christians were maligned and misrepresented
before the civic authorities, Justin addressed an *Apology* to the
Emperor on their behalf. In it he gives a full description of a
Sunday Service of worship in which these Christians engaged.

The outline of this act of worship appeared as follows:

(a) Lessons are read from the memoirs of the Apostles (i.e. the
Gospels) and from the Prophets as long as time permits.

(b) The President (προεστώς) gives instruction based upon
what has been read.

(c) Common prayers are offered "for ourselves, for him who
has received illumination (i.e. for the person baptized) and
for all others everywhere." All are standing.

(d) The Kiss of Peace.

(e) Bread and wine and water are brought to the President.

(f) Eucharistic Prayer. The President "offers up praise and
glory to the Father of all things through the name of the Son
and the Holy Spirit and gives thanks (εὐχαριστίαν) at length for
that we have been accounted worthy of these things by Him."
All the people say "Amen."

(g) Communion. "Those who are called by us Deacons give
of the bread and wine and water, which have been dedicated
with the εὐχαριστία, to everyone present, to partake of them;
and they carry them also to those not present."

(h) Voluntary contributions of money are made to the President by the more prosperous for the relief of the orphans,
sick, widows, poor, and needy."[27]

From these writings, which are representative of the period
A.D. 65 to 150, and from the evidences we examined before,
some general conclusions may be drawn about the worship
practices of the early Church:

(a) From the *Didaché* we conclude that the Eucharist was the
highest act of Christian worship. It was observed every Lord's
Day and was marked by thanksgiving and a vivid sense of
communion and fellowship. The center of this unity was Christ,
and the experience of his presence was the key to this fellow-

ship. Also, in this writing, there is a glimmer of an authentic sacramental note: the bread and wine becoming outward and visible signs of an inward and spiritual grace. The eschatological emphasis is there in the reference to the gathering in of the Church into God's Kingdom. Pliny's *Letter* indicates the corporate nature of the Sunday act of worship. Common praise was offered to Christ and it was done sometimes in an antiphonal ceremony: "Carmen Christo quasi Deo dicere *secum invicem.*"

(b) The pattern of worship in Justin Martyr's service was a complete fusion of the service of the synagogue and the Eucharist. This became the basic form around which the services of Christendom were later built. The Holy Scriptures were read and instruction given. The bread and wine were an integral part of the service, consecrated by prayer and not by the recitation of a formula, and the celebrant stood behind the Holy Table from which the elements were given to the people as they communed. As in the *Didaché,* prerequisites to communion were defined as contrition for sin and love to the brethren. Similarly in Justin Martyr, there were essentials for partaking: belief in the doctrines taught, in baptism, and in Christian living.

These were some of the things the Reformers felt were rightfully our heritage from early Christian worship, and their effort to restore them marked the more positive aspects of the Protestant Reformation.

From the Reformation Churches

Before we examine the contribution made to Reformed worship by the Reformation Churches on the European continent, we must note briefly some of the unfortunate trends that began to appear in the second century and that became eventually those wrongs in the Medieval Church which the Reformers declared against. The chief abuses which the Protestant movement sought to remove or set right were: the doctrine of transubstantiation and the clerical power it implied; the mechanical interpretation of salvation by works; the substitution of tradition for Gospel and the Church for the Bible, thus eliminating the right of private judgment in matters of faith and morals; and the exclusion of the laity from sharing in common worship by denying their participation in the Eucharist and by the absence of the vernacular in the liturgy. Since ritual, insofar as it expresses a belief, has its foundation in doctrine, the re-thinking of the whole statement of the Christian faith by the reformers was bound to result in radical changes in their forms of worship.

It must be remembered that none of these abuses appeared suddenly as fully grown errors in the story of the Medieval Church, but were the end-product or outcome of ideas that were taking shape even as early as the end of the second century. Indeed many of them were in germ form in the thinking of some of the greatest Christian historians and theologians of that time who otherwise left an influence for good upon the Church's beliefs and life.

It is not intended that this book should sketch the complex formulation of the Eucharistic doctrine of the Medieval Church; such an account could fill many volumes. Moreover, a student of the history of Christian doctrine who acquaints himself with the writings of Irenaeus, Tertullian, Hippolytus, and Cyprian, will discover evidences of the germinal ideas that shaped this rite and will be able to identify and sort out the many pagan embellishments that were accumulated along the way. He will see in the writings of Irenaeus,[28] for example, the gradual growth into ascendancy of the concept of sacrifice in the Eucharist and how the focus of the people's offering was changed from charity to the presenting of the Host to God. This latter idea came from pagan sources outside Judaism where the presentation of a loyal heart was considered insufficient, and therefore by means of the Eucharistic prayer the elements themselves were now given to God. Almost simultaneously the belief arose that God met this earthly gift with a divine response by incorporating within it a new and mysterious quality, a forecast of the doctrine of transubstantiation.

Into this picture Cyprian brought eventually the Old Testament idea of the priesthood and from this new union declared that in the Eucharist "the priest is surely a true vicegerent of Christ who imitates that which Christ did; and he offers a true and full sacrifice to God the Father, if he begins to offer as he sees Christ himself is offered."[29] Not only was this the outgrowth of an idea that was hinted at in the writings of Tertullian,[30] but it displaced the consecration by prayer in the Eucharist with the use of a formula. "The bread which Christ took and distributed to his disciples he made his Body, saying (dicendo) 'This is My Body.'" With this belief in the elements as the real Body and blood of Christ, the adoration of the Host emerged very easily and the offering of it to God as the Church's oblation, suggested earlier in the Eucharistic prayer of Hippolytus, naturally followed. D. H. Hislop, in commenting on this prayer, said, "Here in embryo is the Roman thought."[31]

This was only a step from identifying the Mass with the sacrifice of Calvary which the priest, by the power vested in him, presents anew on each occasion as a propitiation for the sins of all Christians, living or dead. Adolf Harnack[32] indicates how these various strands of liturgical thought appeared more fully in Cyprian: "Cyprian first clearly associated the specific offering of the Lord's Supper with the specific priesthood; Cyprian first declared the *passio Domini,* and also the *sanguis Christi,* and the *dominica hostia* the object of the eucharistic offering. In this way he reaches the idea of the priestly re-enacting of the Sacrifice of Christ." So, by the time of Gregory the Great (A.D. 550–604), it was generally accepted and believed, as R. M. Adamson suggests, that "the oblation of Christ's body is constantly repeated by the priest."[33]

The Middle Ages was a favorable time for the growth of new superstitions and the development of strange traditions. With the break-up of the Roman Empire all kinds of pagan beliefs and rites flowed into the vacuum, and the tendency was to find religion in ceremonial rather than in the apprehension of the truth in the face of Jesus Christ. To quote Adamson again: "The Christ of history receded into the background and the Christ of dogma was more and more obtruded."[34] In A.D. 1215, the Doctrine of Transubstantiation was officially recognized by ecclesiastical sanction and declared as an imperative dogma by the Fourth Lateran Council. The exact wording was: "Jesus Christ is at once priest and sacrifice, whose body and blood are truly contained in the sacrifice of the altar under the appearance of bread and wine, the bread being transubstantiated into the body and the wine unto the blood by divine power."

Peter Lombard and Thomas Aquinas, leading Schoolmen of the twelfth and thirteenth centuries, attempted to vindicate intellectually the accumulation of the Church's doctrines. At the same time other changes were taking place and new ceremonial was appearing: the discontinuance of child-communion, the denial of the cup to the laity, the beginning of processions in adoration of the Host and Corpus Christi Feasts. Masses increased in number and variety, and the opportunity of paying for them was introduced. This became one of the major issues that precipitated the protest and witness of the Reformation.

Now the agencies that brought the reformed principles to their fullest expression in the sixteenth century had their forerunners in the thinking of men whose influence is not always given the credit it deserves. As Thomas Leishman wrote, "The Reformation is not to be thought of as a single event. . . . It did not come like the sudden outburst of a tropical sunrise to awake a slumbering world."[35] Ratramnus, for example, a priest of Corbie and a native of Picardy, wrote a treatise *De Corpore et sanguine Domini* about the middle of the ninth century, whom Doumergue names as "the spiritual predecessor of Calvin." Indeed Joseph Martin, in a work called *Ratramne-une conception de la Cène au neuvième siècle*, acclaims him the creator of the Protestant doctrine of the Eucharist. Although his writings remained unnoticed for several centuries, yet they can be said to have come into their own in the teachings of Calvin and were regarded as an embarrassment to the Roman Catholic Church. To illustrate this, here is a short paragraph from Taylor's translation:

> Yet let it not be thought . . . that in the mystery of the Sacrament, the Body and Blood of the Lord are not received by the faithful, for faith receiveth that which it believeth, not what the eye beholdeth. It is spiritual meat, and spiritual drink; spiritually doth it feed the soul, and giveth life, which shall satisfy for ever, as our Saviour saith himself, when commending to us this mystery, 'It is the Spirit which quickeneth: the flesh profiteth nothing.'[36]

Among fourteenth and early fifteenth century personalities whose thinking and witness foreshadowed the greater events of the Reformation were John Wycliffe, John Huss, and Girolamo Savonarola. In 1380 Wycliffe made a sharp attack upon the doctrine of transubstantiation and the echo of it reached Huss in Bohemia at the beginning of the fifteenth century. The latter died at the stake for his convictions on July 6, 1415, and thereby confirmed Rome's intolerance of any and all opposition, which has continued with unabated zeal even to this day. Savonarola's revolt against Papal authoritarianism influenced Luther in Germany. Erasmus' translation of the New Testament exerted not a little influence when it opened up the original writings of the Bible and particularly what was the early complexion of the Sacraments.

The first major reformer was Martin Luther (1483–1546). Although his ideas about public worship have never been clarified satisfactorily, yet his contribution to Protestant liturgy has been considerable as a result of the principles he held and the changes he supported. It must be noted that Luther "was chary of putting forward constructive suggestions for the re-forming of the cultus."[37] His views were quite flexible and his attitudes rather liberal. These were due to his conviction that unless the Scriptures definitely forbade a liturgical form there was no need to abandon or suppress it. To quote Moffatt again,

"His view of the Word did not involve any fixed or explicit form of worship. . . . So long as the heart of the Word was soundly preserved, he cared comparatively little how the faithful in his own communion expressed their devotion, though he pled for a reasonable uniformity."[38] And again, "Luther sometimes saw what had to be done rather than how it should be done."[39] As a result he has suffered from two main criticisms that have been made of his liturgical effort: that his *Formula missae* (1523) and his *Deutsche Messe* (1526) were inferior in quality to Diebold Schwarz's Strassburg rite and less creative than later Lutheran formularies in other national traditions; and that in his pains to reform the Mass rather than abolish it, he leaned inadvertently towards the traditional Roman point of view and therefore his doctrine of consubstantiation was not radically different from the ancient concept of transubstantiation.

On the other hand, as Maxwell points out,[40] Luther's greatest contribution to our liturgical tradition was the restoration of the idea of fellowship to the act of worship, the implications of which were a mortal thrust at the abuses of the Roman Mass, as his *Babylonish Captivity* (1520) bears out. With this new emphasis upon fellowship, the purpose of the Mass was changed and its inherent nature came under careful review. It followed that the only satisfactory celebration would have to be in the language of the people and include some instruction in the form of a homily. The Mass as a repetition of Christ's sacrifice was denied once and for all and its affiliation with a mechanical system of merit and good words was repudiated. Luther declared,

The third bondage (the first was Communion in one kind; the second was transubstantiation as an article of faith) of this same Sacrament is that abuse of it—and by far the most impious—by which it has come about that at this day there is no belief in the Church more generally received or more firmly held than that the Mass is a good work and a sacrifice. This abuse has brought in an infinite flood of other abuses, until faith in the Sacrament has been utterly lost, and they have made this divine Sacrament a mere sub-

ject of traffic, huckstering, and money-getting contracts. Hence
communions, brotherhoods, suffrages, merits, anniversaries, memo-
rials, and other things of that kind are bought and sold in the
Church, and made the subject of bargains and agreements; and the
entire maintenance of priests and monks depends on these things.[41]

The second major reformer was Huldreich Zwingli (1484–
1531), whose influence upon the Reformation would have been
more permanent and far-reaching had he not swung towards
what amounted to a radically negative position. His chief liturgical treatises were *The Attack upon the Canon of the Mass*
(1523) and *Clear Explanation of the Lord's Supper* (1526).
Traditionally he has been treated as mildly suspect and his service of worship discounted for its barrenness and lack of both
imagination and a sense of the Church as the community of
God's people. Two strong influences upon Zwingli can account
for his point of view. In the matter of temperament he was
colored by the rationalism of Erasmus. The elements of pathos
and devotion, which are the stuff of human fellowship, were
less in him than the desire for simplicity, clarity, and literal-
ism. The other influence was in the area of interpretation and
came from the thinking of Cornelius Hoen (or Honius), a
Dutch lawyer, who himself had been stirred by Wessel Gans-
fort's treatise on the Lord's Supper, *De Sacramento eucharis-
tiae*. Hoen's famous letter on the meaning of the declaration,
"This is my Body," which he sent to Luther in 1521, was a new
insight for Zwingli. Later he wrote of "a letter of a certain
learned and pious Dutchman, which has now been published
anonymously. Here I found the word 'is' to mean 'signifies.'
The figure of speech, therefore, was hidden in the word "is.' "[42]
The word of Scripture became then for Zwingli the ultimate
court of appeal, hence the traditionally ornate Eucharist was
displaced by the Lord's Supper as an act of commemoration,
subordinate to preaching. "The Eucharist or Communion or
Lord's Supper," writes Zwingli, "is nothing else than a commemoration, whereby those who firmly believe that they have

been reconciled to the Father by the death and blood of Christ announce this life-giving death, that is, praise it and glory in it and proclaim it."[43] The Lord's Supper was to him "an occasional confessional act"[44] or "an acted sermon"[45] which added nothing to the Word which had been proclaimed.

Zwingli, however, must not be lightly dismissed. Both Farel and Calvin owed much to this Zurich reformer for preparing the way for their later achievements in Geneva, and what is more, "his Communion Liturgy was retained, almost unchanged, in Zurich until 1675."[46]

The most pivotal figure in the worship of the Reformed tradition is, of course, John Calvin (1509–1564). There is the tendency to identify him exclusively with Geneva, and certainly it was there he did his greatest work in building up a Christian edifice where Farel had already pulled down the altars of idolatry.[47] But no full picture of Calvin can be drawn without some reference to his sojourn in Strassburg from 1538 to 1541 and his association there with Martin Bucer.

Just as Calvin's ideas were a kind of *via media* between Luther and Zwingli, so did Bucer appear as a moderate between Zwingli and Calvin. His ideas about eucharistic liturgy may be found in *Nine Propositions Concerning the Holy Eucharist* (1530), and in maturer form later in *Confessions Concerning the Holy Eucharist* (1550). As the leading representative of the Strassburg school, his position regarding the meaning of the Eucharist may be stated in this way: "While the mouth receives the symbols, the bread and wine, the worthy soul receives and feeds upon the reality, the body and blood of Christ. But the unworthy receives the bare elements only."[48] Up till 1530, Schwarz's mass was the most widely used in Strassburg, but from then onwards Bucer's influence became more pronounced and by 1539 a service book, *Psalter mit aller Kirchenübung*, appeared from which the Calvinistic and Scottish liturgies were later derived. Also—and this is of real importance—it was from this German rite that the service arose which was to become eventually the norm for regular Sunday worship in all branches of the Reformed tradition, namely, the eucharistic service with the communion omitted.[49]

While in Strassburg and as a service to the other French exiles there, Calvin had this German rite translated into his native tongue and saw its completion in 1539. On his return to Geneva, a service book, similar to the Strassburg edition, appeared in 1542, called *La Forme de Prières*. Students of Reformed liturgy agree with J. S. Whale's opinion that "there is a clearly traceable relationship all along the line from Schwarz's German Mass of 1524 to *La Forme de Strassburg* (Bucer), to *La Manyère de faire prières* (Strassburg, 1539), to *La Forme* (Calvin, 1542, 1543), to *The Book of Geneva*, and *The Book of Common Order*."[50]

The following is the outline of the service of worship according to Calvin's Genevan Order, 1542:

LITURGY OF THE WORD

Scripture Sentence: Ps. 124:8
Confession of Sins
Prayer for Pardon
Metrical Psalm
Collect for Illumination
Lection
Sermon

LITURGY OF THE UPPER ROOM

Collection of Alms
Intercessions
Lord's Prayer
Preparation of Elements while
Apostles' Creed is sung
Words of Institution
Exhortation

Consecration Prayer
Fraction
Delivery
Communion
Post-Communion Collect
Aaronic Blessing

"The focus of the Reformation of the sixteenth century was the Church's worship."[51] But the changes that occurred in worship came naturally from a prior revolutionary transformation in the field of doctrine. This is more true of Calvin than any other among the Reformers. His *Institutes of the Christian Religion,* which Thomas Leishman called "the most important work in the history of theological science," are the bases of those changes that found expression in concrete acts of worship. Other sources of information are *Tracts Relating to the Reformation* (especially Volume I with "The Necessity of Reforming the Church," a letter addressed to the Emperor Charles V), *La Forme des Prières Ecclesiastiques* and *Le Catechisme de Geneve, Letters of John Calvin* (ed. Bonnet), and A. L. Herminjard's *Correspondance des Reformateurs dans les pays de langue Française.* From a study of these writings we discover what are the main liturgical forms and ideas that we count as our heritage from Calvin and the Genevan Church.

(a) The Calvinistic service is the clearest example of worship based upon the idea of Revelation. At its heart is the principle that God's Word is supreme and that it comes to us with its promise in both preaching and sacraments. Therefore the Word must be proclaimed before the Lord's Supper is observed. The people must receive instruction first—an echo of Luther—so that they may come with minds that understand and with hearts that feel some justification for doing what they do. As Calvin has stated, "There is no use in the sacraments unless the thing which the sign visibly represents is explained in accordance with the Word of God."[52]

(b) Calvin puts the Lord's Supper within the context of

the Word because it is a visible sign of the promises which
that Word declares. He would agree with Olaus Petri, the
Swedish Lutheran Reformer, "Without preaching the Sacraments are of little use." In this emphasis upon the Word *and*
Sacraments in Calvin, we get (a) a restoration of the prophetic
element which the Medieval Church had lost, and (b) a
wholeness to the act of worship which the modern Church
has forfeited. T. H. L. Parker comments, "The Word and the
sacraments are not to be regarded as two separate means of
grace, but as together constituting one means of grace."[53]
Doumergue puts it, "Le culte calviniste est un."[54]

(c) Calvin's service of worship is experienced best within
the framework of an adequate doctrine of the Church. To him
the Church was not a mere aggregation of miscellaneous folk
who met in a customary room on Sunday morning. The worshipping congregation was the Body of Christ. And in this position the influence of Bucer and Strassburg upon him was strong.
For Calvin, it is the Church that worships, not individuals as
isolated entities, but as persons who realize their fullest spiritual potential within the fellowship of God's people. Each
member takes part in the Christian community, and there is
no priestly caste superior to laity, for all believers are one in
their need of grace.

(d) Calvin's idea of God and of man's relationship to him
influenced the complexion and temper of his service of worship. God is sovereign; therefore all glory is due to him. Worship then has a new warrant and takes on a real objectivity.
Our aim is to glorify God. For this, ceremonial is not the
highest medium, because the better we understand and the
more profoundly we adore, the less we require forms and
the nearer we come to Reality. Worship, for Calvin, was essentially a two-sided activity; it was a reciprocal exchange
between God and man. A. M. Fairbairn had this point of view
in mind when he wrote, "In Christian worship a living man
cries unto the living God and the living God speaks respon-
sively to the living man."[55]

(e) In reply to those who discredit the quality of Calvinistic worship on account of its bareness, we must point out that with the Reformers "it was their right as rational and responsible beings to reject all mere human authority in religious matters, to try everything by the standard of God's Word, and to judge for themselves, on their own responsibility, as to the meaning of these statements."[56] Their demand for positive Scriptural sanction swept away all the Medieval ceremonialism and hierarchism which had corrupted the worship of God. In the place of these came the prophetic note, the glow of fellowship, the high sentiments of the psalms and hymns, and that sincerity and dignity, without which no service can be impressive and rich. Calvin's service had unity, also, which is a basic prerequisite of beauty, and a climactic movement that matched the natural aspirations of the human soul.

(f) Calvin's service makes clear and meaningful to us what comes to us in our act of worship, namely, God's grace. Some people, who are uninformed, think of Calvin only as a severe dispenser of decrees of predestination and they associate the liturgical tradition of Geneva with grim reminders of election and condemnation. "The truth is," wrote Herman Bavinck, "that no preacher of the Gospel has ever surpassed Calvin in the free, generous proclamation of the love and grace of God."[57] Now the Reformers defined grace as God's favor shown to men in Jesus Christ and accepted and appropriated by them through faith. It involves therefore a personal relationship between the divine and the human. Deissmann called it "a spiritual fellowship between Christ and his own,"[58] which was clearly what the Reformers had in mind.

Their new definition, moreover, was bound to have its immediate effect upon the nature and form of worship, particularly in the Lord's Supper, where Christ's presence was now proclaimed as an event of grace. This sacrament was a visible sign confirming and clarifying the spiritual benefits the Word declares. It is not, however, in the symbols themselves that we see Christ's work but in the *action:* the breaking of bread and the outpouring of wine. Calvin emphasized the *transaction*[59] of the Lord's Supper as the important matter, but all too often his followers have failed to comprehend it. Forsyth once wrote, "It is not this object, but this act."[60] And this is an action in which persons are involved: Christ is conveyed spiritually to the soul of the believer. Moreover, the integrity of the whole action is vouchsafed by the truth of Christ's promise and by the reality of our Christian experience. We feel Christ's presence, not in any substance, but in power. When the emphasis is upon the substance or the things, the Supper is depersonalized as in the Roman service, where Christ's presence is placed in the elements themselves rather than in the hearts of the believers. In the Lord's Supper in the Reformed tradition God's grace comes to us not from the supper itself, but *with it* as his gift to all who will do his will.

FROM THE SCOTTISH CHURCH

Whatever ritual the Church of Scotland had originally was traceable to Eastern, not Roman sources, and it came by way of Ireland through some monks, of whom St. Columba of Iona was the most celebrated. After Queen Margaret had Romanized the country in the eleventh century, modes of worship were either of two extremes: colorful ceremonial was common in the cathedrals, while in the country parishes, which were in the majority, the services were coarse and poorly administered. Five centuries later the Reformers found more to do than to undo, and hence their task was made easier.

With the removal of the Mass in England, the *Missal* was discarded, but the *Breviary* was retained because it was a useful collection of devotional forms and offices. It became, moreover, the source of the initial prayer book to be used in England, the work of Archbishop Cranmer, which was called the *First Prayer Book of Edward VI* (1549).

This book was the first liturgy used in the Church of Scotland after the Reformation. And while the story of our heritage in worship from the European Reformation, particularly Geneva, involved theological principles and the liturgical forms they created, our legacy from Scotland can be traced more clearly through the growth of the *Book of Common Order*.

Although Roman Catholicism was not officially outlawed until 1560, yet in Scotland "the Lords of the Congregation" (as the Reformers were called) wrote the clause into the first draft of their Solemn League in 1557, "that Common Prayer be read in the parish churches on Sunday, with the Lessons of the New and Old Testaments, conforming to the order of the Book of Common Prayer." The reference was to Edward's *Second Book of Prayer* (revised edition, 1552).

It is interesting to note here how very much the formularies of the Church of England owe to the Continental reformers. The Liturgy of Cologne (1543), on which Bucer and Melanchthon worked so closely, was one of the primary sources of considerable sections of this revised edition of Edward's *Book of Prayer*. "From this Liturgy," wrote Archbishop Laurence, "our offices bear evident marks of having been freely borrowed—liberally imitating, but not servilely copying it." These borrowings included the Baptismal Service, Confession of Sins, Absolution, Post-Communion Thanksgiving, almost all of the Solemnization of Matrimony, and a large part of the Order for the Burial of the Dead.[61] Indeed both Peter Martyr and Martin Bucer, during their professorships at Oxford and Cambridge, were consulted incessantly on points of doctrine and discipline.

Knox, too, during his short ministries in England from 1549 to 1552, prior to his royal chaplaincy, was active in the shaping of the *Book of Prayer*—especially the Communion service, where his opposition to the current interpretation of the "real presence" finally won through. Evidences of the influence of Calvin's Strassburg rite are found in the changes made in Edward's *Second Book* in the preliminary forms of the daily service and in the words of the distribution of the elements in the Lord's Supper.

With Mary Tudor's accession to the English throne in 1553, the Prayer Book was suppressed, and about a thousand exiles fled to the Continent, including John Knox and some two hundred folk who sought refuge in Frankfort. There Knox became the minister of a small congregation which soon became the focal point of liturgical controversy. The civil magistrates gave permission for them to use the French church in the city as long as the French liturgy was observed. The English church group, however, preferred Edward's *Second Book*, while Knox and his party wanted no part of it. This was a forecast in miniature of the struggle between Conformists and Nonconformists that occurred in England later. A temporary peace was achieved through the adoption of a "Liturgy of Compromise," based largely upon the English forms, but sufficiently dissimilar to be acceptable to all the parties concerned. But new immigrations of exiles kept the old issues alive, until Knox decided to withdraw to Geneva (1555), where he became the first minister of a congregation of other English exiles. Here, with the help of Calvin, he drew up a form of service, based largely on original orders framed by Calvin in Frankfort in 1554 and by Whittingham and others before they consented to the "Liturgy of Compromise."

When Queen Mary died (1558), Knox returned to Scotland in early 1559, bringing his Geneva Book with him. In 1560 it was published as the *First Book of Discipline*, and contained ritual for the administration of the Sacraments, marriage ceremony, and the burial of the dead. It was reprinted in Edinburgh in 1564 with some prayers and the Psalter added. In that same year the General Assembly authorized its use in all churches and called it *The Book of Common Order*, although popularly it was known as "Knox's Liturgy." It remained the official liturgy of the Church of Scotland until 1645, when it was superseded by the Westminster *Directory of Worship*.

One of the healthy features of this book, which was due doubtlessly to the Continental reformers, was the generous provision made for the service of praise, so far scarcely admitted into the Anglican ritual. And further, although the prayers in this Genevan Book could not match the quality of Cranmer's style and charm, yet the special services are of the highest order. This is particularly true of the ritual for the celebration of the Lord's Supper, which might serve as a model for any Reformed group.

This establishment of a Liturgy in Scotland was not the end of controversy. It was merely a period of uneasy peace in a long and protracted struggle between English and Scottish ecclesiastical forces, which resulted finally in the ban of the English *Book of Common Prayer* from Scotland. Aggravation was increased by the actions of King James, Elizabeth's successor, who tried to stamp out the spirit of English puritanism and the Scottish presbytery, and to make the latter conform to the model of the English Church. But, as R. H. Story put it, "the Scottish people refused to be coerced despite the King's threats and the bishops' bullying."

Three decades of incidents followed that were marked by constant meddling on the part of the Crown, King James, and his successor, Charles I—with Archbishop Laud always in the wings—in the affairs of the General Assembly, which after one of the royal demands to conform did not meet for twenty years. Charles, however, was inclined to relax on the pressure, but under the fanatical urgings of Laud an attempt was made to impose a "Book of Canons" (1636) officially upon the Scottish Church, with a deadline set for Easter, 1637. Excommunication was threatened upon all who denied the absolute right of the Crown or the *Summum jus* of the *Book of Common Prayer*. Kirk Sessions were to be suppressed and no clerical assemblies permitted without authorization by the Crown. All these things came to a distressing climax in St. Giles Church, Edinburgh, on July 23, 1637, in the now famous Jenny Geddes incident when Laud's Liturgy was first introduced in the place of *The Book of Common Order* which had been used for some seventy years. This was the escape valve that let forth two streams of events—political and ecclesiastical. Politically: the Solemn League and Covenant, the civil war, the beheading of the King, and the protectorate under Oliver Cromwell. Ecclesiastically: the Glasgow Assembly of 1638 which condemned the Book of Canons and Laud's Liturgy; the end of Episcopacy; and the deputizing of the Scottish Commissioners to the Assembly of Divines at Westminster. The eventual outcome was the appearance of *The Directory for Public Worship*, which was authorized by the Long Parliament in 1645 and approved in the same year by the General Assembly.

The attitude of the Church of Scotland for the next two hundred years was quite indifferent as far as any liturgy was concerned and the result was that by the end of the eighteenth century the Scottish services of worship were the barest in Christendom. The sermon was everything. Prayers were dreary and lamentably composed. By the middle of the nineteenth century, however, a liturgical revival began to appear, particularly in the service of praise. After the Secession of 1843, a movement under Dr. Robert Lee showed serious concern for the reform of Scottish worship and sought to restore the recognition of the liturgical forms of the Reformed heritage. Lee met with much opposition, even hostility, but he based his claims upon the liberty of worship guaranteed by the Directory which no Assembly had repealed. The most concrete result of this new stirring over liturgical forms was the founding of the Church Service Society in 1865, the purpose of which was stated as follows:

It is no restless feeling of dissatisfaction with the traditional usages, doctrines, and rites of the Church which has directed general attention to the question of worship; it is rather an earnest desire that the Church's worship should become a more and more comely and perfect vehicle of her devotion, that has led men to inquire wherein it is capable of improvement.[62]

A Euchologion or Book of Prayers was published in 1867 which ran into nine editions and was finally called *The Book of Common Order*, continuing the title of Knox's Liturgy. In the wake of this revival of interest in worship, various books of prayer and order began to appear in the Scottish Church. In 1940, however, under the authority of the General Assembly of the reunited Church of Scotland a new and revised *Book of Common Order* was approved, which contained materials from *Prayers for Divine Service* (1923 and 1929) and the *Book of Common Order* (1928).

In America, Presbyterian worship has been influenced in mood by the Puritan tradition (as we shall see in greater detail in the next section) and in form by the *Directory for Public Worship*. When, in deference to the seventeenth century English Independents, the Scottish Church gave up its *Book of Common Order* in favor of the *Directory,* it forfeited much from its worship tradition, particularly in the role of the congregation in the service and in the quality and subject matter of the prayers. Moreover, the positive suggestions of the *Directory* were frequently overlooked, while the dimensions of some prohibitions were magnified. Among the less happy impressions that found their way across the sea was that Presbyterians were committed to "non-liturgical worship." This superstition persisted, even though as early as 1855 no less a churchman than Charles Hodge recommended "the optional use of a liturgy, or form of public service, having the sanction of the Church."

Books of forms began to appear intermittently in America and some of them, especially those by Hodge and Herrick Johnson, received considerable attention. In 1876, Henry Van Dyke, Sr., then Moderator of the General Assembly, called for some book of forms to be prepared and authorized by the Church. But it was not before 1901 that a definite overture was presented, and, in 1903, a committee appointed. In 1906 the book appeared and was approved by the General Assembly "for voluntary use." Lay opposition to these forms was openly hostile and a concerted effort was made to discharge the committee. But the clergy received the new book warmly and were moved to begin a new era of order and propriety in the worship of the Presbyterian Church in the United States of America.

The first revision of the *Book of Common Worship* was made in 1928 and a major one in 1944. In the Preface, a debt to the Genevan and Scottish traditions is acknowledged in these words:

The movement with the Church looking to the improvement of worship seeks therefore not only to provide the minister with the treasures in thought and expression that are the inheritance of the Church, but to encourage Christian congregations to more active participation in Christian worship, which was the custom in the early Church and is the heritage of the Protestant Reformation.

The Committee has been aided in its work by the publication of helpful treatises on worship and prayer. Within the Reformed Churches there have been important publications which have supplied the Committee with suggestions, forms of expression, and prayers. Among these we mention *The Book of Common Order* of the Church of Scotland, which bears the same name as John Knox's *Book of Common Order*, a book which was in use in Scotland for nearly one hundred years. With the approval of the Church of Scotland the Committee has taken freely from this excellent book, and to the Mother Church, which has given us permission to make use of it as desired, we express our grateful thanks.[63]

From the Puritans

As it was intimated at the conclusion of the last section, the mood and pattern of the worship of the Reformed Churches in America were influenced and shaped by English Puritanism. However, whatever forms are currently used in American Presbyterianism, for example, can be traced to the Scottish Church, although the recognition and use of this liturgy in this country are not many decades old. For years such forms were designated as being "optional" in order to appease opposing factions within the denomination. Puritan influences marked more plainly the worship of Congregationalists and Baptists also, while the Methodists combined threads of both Anglican and Free Church traditions. To understand the char-

acter of the worship of these churches and to evalute properly
the heritage they have bequeathed to us, we must go back
to sixteenth and seventeenth century England and review
briefly those forces that gave birth to the Free Church tradition.

The Reformation in England was in the beginning a political
matter. As F. M. Powicke put it, "The one definite thing which
can be said about the Reformation in England is that it was
an act of State."[64] Henry VIII's break with Rome, however,
gave a tremendous impetus to the spirit of inquiry and of re-
sistance to arbitrary, especially ecclesiastical, power. There
developed, therefore, a wide "grass roots" movement which
both royalty and establishment sought to direct into the area
of their own particular interests. This movement gave rise to
Puritanism, one of the most powerful influences in English
thought and life since the beginnings of the Reformation.

Whatever aberrations were spawned by this movement, the
opinion can never be gainsaid that it was basically a struggle
for religious liberty. The initial herald, as we indicated earlier
in this chapter, was John Wycliffe (1320–1384). In his *Westminster Assembly* (p. 3), A. F. Mitchell wrote, "English could
produce no Luther in the sixteenth century simply because it
had its Luther already in the fourteenth." Wycliffe's primary
contention was for the recognition of the supreme authority
of Scripture. And his followers, the Lollards or "evangelical
men," went up and down England, proclaiming the gospel
and becoming the conscience of their generation. Indeed some
of them were the first Puritan martyrs, although this derisive
name had not as yet been coined. No spectacular leader, no
Calvin or Zwingli, was the spearhead of religious reform in
England, but a whole succession of nameless persons from
Wycliffe to William Tyndale were forerunners of the later
and more cataclysmic events. As a result of their influence the
Reformation in England became eventually noble and brilliant
at a time when the European movement was succumbing to
scholasticism.

Broadly speaking, the Reformation in England resolved itself

into two branches: the Puritan party which adhered to the
XXXIX Articles; and the ecclesiastical group which embraced
The Book of Common Prayer. The Puritans were not a separate
organization, but were actually a party in church and state.
Article VI was one of their essential tenets; they took their
stand upon it over against the prelates. It read:

Holy Scripture containeth all things necessary to salvation, so
that whatever is not read therein, nor may be proved thereby, is
not to be required of any man that it should be believed as an
article of faith, or be thought requisite or necessary to salvation.

This became the point at issue in the controversy. The ecclesiastical hierarchy considered the Bible as being authoritative only in matters of doctrine and ethical conduct. The
Puritans, on the other hand, contended that it was the indis-
putable source for patterns of church government, worship,
discipline, as well as for conduct. In this they echoed the
point of view of John Calvin. And Calvin's Geneva was to
lend impetus to the Puritans for further Reformation according to the Word of God.

How did Calvinism get to England? In several ways: exiles
who had sought haven in Europe during the persecutions
under Edward VI eventually returned; later exiles like Whittingham and Coverdale, who fled England during the reign of
Mary, came back after the accession of Elizabeth; and, as
was mentioned earlier in this chapter, distinguished Reformers,
among them Martin Bucer and Peter Martyr, who were invited
by Cranmer to the Regius Chairs of Divinity at Oxford and
Cambridge, presented their interpretations in person. In Scotland, through the influence of Knox, the Puritan position was
stated in the Scots Confession, Article XIX:

As we believe and confess the Scriptures of God sufficient to in-
struct and make the man of God perfect, so do we affirm and avow
the authority of the same to be of God, neither to depend on men
or angels. We affirm, therefore, that such as allege the Scripture
to have no other authority but that which it has received from the
church, to be blasphemous against God and injurious to the true

church which always hears and obeys the voice of her own spouse and pastor, but takes not upon her to be mistress over the same.

The cleavage in England was much deeper: the Anglican group based the canon of Scripture on the authority of church tradition, while the Puritans "lodged the authority of the Bible in itself."

The first great leader of English Puritanism was Thomas Cartwright; the last, we might say, was Richard Baxter, whose *Reformation of the Liturgy,* presented at the Savoy Conference, 1661, was voted down. Cartwright, who was Lady Margaret Professor of Divinity at Cambridge, denounced the Church of England in extreme terms and was deposed from his teaching post in 1570. He was responsible for the second Puritan manifesto to Parliament, *The Second Admonition.* This paper outlined a truly Reformed church in liturgy and government, according to the Genevan tradition. It received short shrift from the forces of the Establishment, although it did result in the founding of the first Presbyterian church at Wandsworth in 1572. Three great principles of Reformation thinking and witness were evident in these Puritan manifestoes: (a) Justification by faith alone; (b) Salvation by grace alone; (c) The Authority of the Word of God alone.

(a) Although Justification by Faith was the keystone of Luther's reforms, yet he and the Calvinists differed in their interpretation of it. Basically it was a matter, with both groups, of justification by faith *versus* works. But the Calvinists went a step further and emphasized also the second principle— salvation by grace alone. While the Lutherans made assurance of the very essence of faith, the Calvinists made a distinction between simple justification by faith and the assurance of faith which results from growth in grace. The Puritans fell in with the Calvinists by urging that simple justification by faith should develop into the realization of the assurance of salvation, which meant not merely a turning away from sin but the appropriation of holiness in all areas of life. This accounted for the ethical activism of Puritanism, allegorized in John

Bunyan's *The Pilgrim's Progress* and *Holy War*. It found expression also in the Puritan legalism regarding the Sabbath and daily religious disciplines. Indeed the writings of Richard Baxter and the sermons of Samuel Smith were eagerly read and taken as concrete outlines for domestic religion.

There have always been those who have criticized the Puritans for legalism akin to Pharisaism, but their desire for living and vital communion with God by a growing faith offset any tendency to capitulate to the Continental scholasticism of the seventeenth century. Indeed they contributed in no small way to the covenant theology of Holland; and to the British and American way of life they gave a strong and upright moral quality which has been a real force for good through the centuries.

(b) Salvation by divine grace alone over against the machinery of church and Sacraments or human media was a second Calvinistic tenet adopted by the Puritans. It found particular expression in the writings of Baxter and Cartwright who emphasized the prevenient grace of God as the sole source of redemption. They argued that this grace of God in the heart should show itself in an experience of grace in life in the form of renewed moral character. For them the grace of God was "an intensely practical grace"—operating in experience, a grace of the Christian life.

(c) The third and most prominent principle in the Puritan manifesto was the Authority of the Word of God. From Calvin, and in England from Wycliffe and Tyndale, the Puritans "made the Holy Spirit speaking in the Bible the sole authoritative interpreter of the Bible and affirmed that God alone was the Lord of conscience, speaking in his Word directly to the believer as the only sovereign and infallible authority."[65] They were forced into this position because they were caught in the struggle between the authority of the Bible on the one hand and the authority of the ecclesiastics on the other. And the latter grew progressively more insistent through the influence of a succession of powerful church figures, including

Whitgift, Bancroft, and finally Laud. The Puritans rose through Cartwright, Owen, Goodwin, and others, and their aspirations found ultimate expression in the Westminster Divines. The issue is stated clearly by Horton Davies: "Roughly the established clergy accepted Luther's doctrine of the authority of the Bible, while the Puritans accepted Calvin's conception of the authority of the Scriptures. The Puritan said that if the Bible is binding on one issue, it is binding on all issues. He could see only inconsistency in the attempt of the established clergy to regard the Bible as authoritative in matters of belief, but not binding in matters of government and worship."[66]

The argument gravitated easily to the area of worship, where it can be said again that generally the Puritans were close to the Genevan tradition, while the Anglicans followed the Lutheran conception of the authority of the Bible and were prepared therefore to accept any forms not specifically forbidden in Scripture. At the center of the debate was *The Book of Common Prayer*. Now the Puritans were not unalterably opposed to such a book, because, after all, the Reformed churches on the Continent had service books, and John Knox introduced *The Book of Common Order* into Scotland. What the Puritans actually wanted was *to purify The Book of Common Prayer* from what they called "Romish ceremonies"—use of vestments, kneeling at the altar to receive the Sacrament, the cross in Baptism, the ring in marriage, and the various responses and forms of prayer. And particularly it was the *imposition* of these forms and customs the Puritans raged against. Indeed it was for this reason that the Westminster Divines produced A *Directory of Worship* rather than a liturgy. They feared the dangers of imposition and knew the advantages of spontaneity and flexibility which a directory permitted.

The Puritan emphases in worship may be summed up then as follows: free prayer in opposition to all formalism and imposed ceremonial; no recognition of the festivals of the Christian year (contrary to Calvin's point of view); the centrality of the sermon as the declaration of God's saving truth

to his people, as opposed to *The Book of Common Prayer*
which encouraged a *reading* rather than a *preaching* ministry;
the expansion of sainthood to include every servant of Christ
according to the New Testament conception; opposition to
private sacraments because this suggested that salvation was
identified primarily with their operation apart from the fellowship of the church; religion was not merely a matter for
stated days or to be circumscribed by sacred rites, but everyone must at all times and in all places, "do justly, love mercy,
and walk humbly with God." To practice and realize these
principles, theirs was the plea of John Milton, the classic
Puritan writer, "Give me the liberty to know, to utter, and
to argue freely according to conscience, above all liberties"
(*Areopagitica,* 1644).

Out of the Puritan movement there came the mood and
shape of the worship of several of the leading denominations
of the Western world: Congregational, Presbyterian, Baptist,
Churches of Christ, and the Methodists—the latter, however,
only in the sense that liturgically they combine the Anglican
tradition with Puritan emphases. As Einar Molland wrote recently, "Methodism has always possessed two traditions, the
one non-liturgical and the other which regards fixed forms of
prayer as of value."[67]

1. *Congregational*

It is not our intention in this small volume to outline the
complex development of the history of the Puritan movement
that resulted in the creation of the Free Churches in England
and their translation to the new world by the New England
colonists. Readers are referred to the scholarly writings of H.
W. Clark, Horton Davies, B. L. Manning, E. A. Payne, A. Peel,
and F. J. Powicke, and others.

As Maxwell has pointed out, the early non-conformist or free
worship in England drew its character from the Genevan
Forme of Prayers, which was later loosely called Knox's Lit-

urgy. The local liturgical controversy among the English exiles at Frankfort marked the beginning of the cleavage between Puritan and Anglican types of worship. The Puritans, moreover, developed eventually into two schools, Presbyterian and Independent (Congregational), the division being more of a matter of polity than of theological or liturgical conviction. Until the appearance of *The Westminster Directory*, the services of both groups were marked by freedom and simplicity, with *The Forme of Prayers* providing merely a shadowy framework. And since the Directory prescribed no forms or content for the liturgy, but was what its title suggested, a compendium of methods, Congregational worship from the seventeenth to the nineteenth centuries was wide in variety and short on meaning. Towards the end of the nineteenth century, however, liturgical revival began to appear, but its development has been spotty; as a result the worship of Congregational churches both in England and America has ranged from the highly liturgical to the barest simplicity. One of the most encouraging facts has been the appearance in recent times of several service manuals, *The Book of Congregational Worship,* by the Congregational Union of England and Wales, and *A Book of Worship for Free Churches,* by the General Council of Congregational Christian Churches in America. Although these books are marked by borrowings from many sources, including *The Book of Common Prayer,* they are indicative happily of a long overdue revival of interest and good intentions.

The peculiar genius of Congregational worship has come from belief in and recognition of "the free and active movement of the Spirit." But the frequent interpretation of this as amounting to no more than spontaneous expression has conspired against the better things the Puritan heritage bequeathed: communion with God in prayer, the reverent learning of his will by reading the Scriptures, the exposition and application of that revelation to the conscience by preaching; and the offering of praise and thanksgiving to God in sacred song. As a result of these emphases, certainly no one can dep-

recate the high quality and reputation attained by Congregational preaching — Parker, Dale, Jowett, Morgan — nor the
splendid contribution it has made to Christian hymnody—Ainsworth, Watts, and Doddridge—nor its close identification of the
Church with the life of the Christian community. Nevertheless
its act of worship can never have a distinctive form until and
unless its shape is created by or is the product of theological
meaning. It is not enough to capture the mood of the Reformers in worship or to parallel their insistence upon including
or rejecting this or that item. The act of worship must have
unity and movement that come from a theological basis which
alone gives meaning to what we say and do in God's House.

2. *Baptist*

If religious individualism be a unique characteristic of the
Reformation, the Baptists can lay claim to be its greatest
expression. John Smyth, a Cambridge man, withdrew in 1605
from the Church of England and after a short pastorate in a
Separatist Church at Gainsborough he left for Holland where
he came under Mennonite influence. Eventually he and a
group of his followers decided that infant baptism was untrue
and they sought to be re-baptized. Hence the name "Ana-
Baptist." After Smyth's death in 1612, some of his adherents
were absorbed by Mennonites while others under the leadership of Thomas Helwys returned to England and settled in
London. Helwys insisted upon believer's baptism so strongly
that he appeared to make it the *sine qua non* of salvation.
Other little churches with a similar persuasion sprang up in
England, although the history of their origin and development
continued to be obscure. Some traffic continued intermittently
with the Mennonites in Holland, but difficulties arose over
the interpretation of church and state relations and eventually
all comity between the two groups petered out.

Baptist churches in England gravitated towards either of
two groups: the General Baptists who became Arminian in

their theology; and the Particular Baptists who were Calvinistic, and therefore more directly Puritan in outlook and temperament. While the latter have always expressed strong
aversions to formal creeds and to prescribed forms of worship,
their convictions have not been without considerable merit in
the broad stream of Free Church worship. With the coming
of Roger Williams to America and the establishing of a Baptist
Church in Providence, Rhode Island, in 1638, three distinctive
marks of Baptist thought appeared in the character of their
worship.

The idea of a covenant church: Contrary to the Anglican
idea which was a parochial concept of the Church, Smyth
maintained that two or more believers could unite by covenant
with each other and with God to form a true church. Theirs was
a "gathered church," as Horton Davies describes it,[68] "a closely-
knit community of men and women covenanting together in
holiness." This concept had definite implications for their worship. Their desire for a covenant, i.e., "an engagement of the
heart," made them averse to adopting historic or written
creeds. Indeed the democratic character of their worship allowed no place for any prescribed forms. The Church was a
family group where "homeliness" was preferred to the proprieties of ritual or creed. And within such a context, extemporary prayer and the absence of a set order of worship became
the natural expression of the reality of inner experience; even
the Eucharist was called the Communion Service, the fellowship of individual believers with one another and with their
Lord.

Salvation by personal faith in Christ: With such a strong
emphasis upon the need for a warm, personal relationship
with Christ, much of Baptist worship was directed towards
edification. Preaching therefore as instruction and for decision
claimed a central place. Since the aim of worship was the
building up of personal faith and of man's conscious relationship with God, even the reading of scripture was accompanied
by a running commentary. This meant that Baptist worship

has been low in devotional power which is invariably the result when "all that he (the worshipper) seeks from his worship is the moral instruction, emotional life, and revival fervor supplied in the sermon."[69]

Appeal to Scripture: From the beginning the Baptists have been a Bible-loving denomination. Although their baptism of believers has been unique (Disciples of Christ also), yet it arose from the general Puritan disposition to appeal to Scripture over against the tradition of the church. In this appeal to the New Testament, for example, the believer immersed and rising from the water in baptism recalled the death and resurrection of Christ: a conception of this rite, apart from all the traditional arguments for and against, has provided Baptists with a distinct edge over the confusion that exists today in interpretations among other denominations, particularly the Presbyterians. This emphasis upon Scripture had two further expressions: in preaching and in missionary zeal. Great Biblical preaching, however, associated with the names of Robert Hall, Alexander MacLaren, and C. H. Spurgeon in the nineteenth century, suffered eclipse in the twentieth from the popularity of the topical and life-situation sermons among American Baptists, particularly in the distinguished preaching of Harry Emerson Fosdick. Baptists have taken seriously the mandate of Matthew 28:19, 20, and their missionary movement from William Carey onwards has been phenomenal in its breadth and unflagging in its enthusiasm.

These characteristics of Baptist thought and practice have been accompanied by a strong undercurrent of freedom of conscience which has made them advocates of religious liberty wherever they have gone. However, their indifference to tradition and their all too literal interpretation of the priesthood of believers have produced an informal type of worship that lacks reverence and devotion, a Communion Service that is Zwinglian at best, and a "soul liberty" that is incompatible with any sense of the church as a spiritual organism.

3. *Methodist*

It is more than passing strange that in a volume of some 200 pages on Methodism in L. P. Jacks' series *The Faiths,* there is no section dealing with worship. Indeed the word "worship" does not appear in the index. Could it be that form and tradition were erased completely by the forward surge of evangelical freedom?

The Puritans were the forerunners of Methodism, although the former were well dead before the Wesleys and Whitfield began their witness and work. J. R. Green once said that "Puritanism won its spiritual victory in the Wesleyan Movement." Like the Reformation itself, Methodism began as a movement within the established church, but its eventual form and status were a new denomination bearing the marks of both its Anglican and Puritan ancestry. In America, however, it played the role of the pioneer, and as its saddlebag preachers moved West with the frontier, both their worship and testimony were cast into the simplicities the environment demanded. "His Book was the Bible, his study Wesley, his guide the Discipline."

The only piece of liturgy that can be classified as a prescribed order in the Methodist churches in America is the Order for the Lord's Supper. John Wesley, unlike clergymen of the Free Churches in England, was not antagonistic towards *The Book of Common Prayer;* it was merely a revised form of it that he sent to the American Church for its adoption in 1784. Two factors, however, were against its general use: there were the exigencies of the frontier and the Coke-Asbury dispute which seemed to be just another threat to America's crusade for liberty. Consequently, the General Conference prepared as a substitute a Discipline, and as Bishop Harmon put it, "The Book of Methodism, instead of a *Prayer Book,* became a Discipline—not *ordered worship,* but ordered *life and activity.*" And again, "It was thus a peculiar twist of fate that Methodism *threw away* the Sunday Service, and *kept* the Occasional Services."[70]

The characteristics therefore that came to the fore in American Methodist worship are those more akin to Puritan influences than to Anglican tradition, although the latter appears clearly in the Order for the Lord's Supper. "The gospel of God's free grace in Christ"[71] has been the watchword of Methodism and the seriousness of this emphasis has given to this denomination evangelistic enthusiasm, piety, and a sense of mission to the "unchurched and unsaved." Its worship, like the Baptists, stresses fellowship, spiritual experience, and lay leadership, and as a result wide variety exists in the shape of Methodist services. "Christianity is a movement rather than a system; it is a spirit, not a form. . . . Growing out of a liturgical church, Methodism has felt free to retain or to discard so much of its inherited forms as seemed wise. . . ." (*Ritual,* "Foreword," 1932). Methodists are accustomed to free prayer in their worship; they have a more enthusiastic service of praise than any of the Free Churches (Charles Wesley wrote 6,500 hymns); and they emphasize the need for good preaching, although unfortunately today the desire to sound practical has crowded out the more qualitative presentation of Christian doctrine.

Today the American churches which were marked most deeply by the Puritan tradition are confronted with a twofold challenge: a revival of interest in worship among the laity and the necessity of channeling this impulse towards fruitful ends without losing the distinctive qualities of their heritage. This will involve learning, interpretation, and re-construction.

From the early Church we inherited a pattern of worship that was theologically meaningful and Biblical in character. When its efficacy was about to be lost through rigid ecclesiastical control and through its being made the means to an institutional end, the Reformation retrieved it for us. The Word and Sacrament were properly oriented again; and the grace of God was no longer controlled by legal processes. Moreover, this was basically a theological reformation which the old

forms could no longer contain or stultify and which inter-
jected the prophetic note into the Church's witness, gave a new
motivation to worship (God's glory), and framed a new concept of what the Church is. As Bernard Manning put it, "To
Geneva belongs the glory of re-stating the meaning of church-
manship: Christ's Kingdom not of this world, Christ's crown
rights in His Kingdom—these things began to have meaning
again."[72]

Concomitant with the forms and devotion of the Scottish
tradition, we became heirs also of the spirit of English Puritanism with its rebellion against the dictates and pressures of an
established religion. But, upon receiving this gift, in more
than a few ways we failed to separate the whole grain from
the chaff. To be sure, the Puritan strategy of judging and
measuring everything by the Word of God gave a sign of
authority to their witness and worship and marked it with
simplicity and spirituality. Unfortunately, however, in general
the rule was all too rigidly applied, and produced a bareness
in their worship by which imagination was discouraged, a
tendency to cater to hearing at the expense of seeing, and an
eagerness to toss out indiscriminatively the legacies of the
centuries. Bible *versus* tradition is invariably a mistake. Bible
and tradition is workable while the latter is under the constant
examination of the former.

Further, the renewed emphasis upon preaching wrote great
chapters in the story of the Reformed witness, especially
preaching that appealed to both reason and conscience and
called for a verdict from the hearer. Yet, whenever the emphasis upon preaching was allowed to over-ride everything
else, the devotional side of worship became improverished.
Or, we may look at it in this way: this new flexibility in the
pattern of worship was an advantage for the expression of
powerful personalities, but had in it two dangers: worship became minister-centered; extemporary prayers in the hands of
the incompetent lapsed either into platitudes or devotional
anarchy.

No one will cease to give praise for the positive contribution of the Puritan movement: its legacy of religious liberty; its re-emphasis upon the nature of God's grace as the Reformers interpreted it; its missionary zeal; its glowing chapters in the history of preaching and in the story of hymnody; its challenge to a personal relationship with the living Christ and its translation into disciplines for daily experience. But in the matter of worship, a new situation now calls for careful re-thinking of the way by which we have come and the things which ordinarily we have done in the accepted ways. Some say that people do not worship today because their faith is anemic and superficial. The contrary, Arthur J. Gossip holds to be more true. People have little faith because they do not know how to worship; they are untutored in the true meaning of worship and the indispensables that go into its making; they have not been shown the proper co-ordination between preaching and worship. Our heritage from the Puritans will be of little profit unless we determine to give to this fresh interest in worship a frame of reference that is both Biblical and theological. This will be our task in the next chapter.

PART III

Preaching and Worship

5

Preaching within the
Context of Worship

The revival of enthusiasm for religion during the past few decades has *generally* been accompanied by a deepening concern for the nature and forms of contemporary worship. "Public worship," writes J. D. Benoît, "is one of the burning questions of the day."[1] This concern, however, is not limited to any one denomination or group, but embraces even those branches of the Christian Church hitherto regarded, both by tradition and choice, as liturgically immutable. Indeed some of the most creative and fruitful discussions of liturgical reform are taking place within the Reformed and Roman Churches in Europe, particularly in France and Switzerland. And the value and permanency of these reforms are assured by the happy fact that this liturgical movement is accompanied by, and indeed issues from, an equally vigorous theological revival. For, after all, Christian worship is the expression of the faith and belief of those engaged in it.

In America too there are definite signs of ferment in the field of worship, but much of the thinking and doing in this area to this date has tended unfortunately to focus upon peripheral matters. Some preachers have become eager advocates of liturgical improvement, but in their zeal they have confused the addition of decorative frills and embellishments with those revisions in the act of worship that should occur by theological sanction. The setting up of extra candles, antependia, fading lights, and other ecclesiastical "make-up" indicates they have been overlooking right content of worship in favor of meaningless psychological devices. Howard Hageman, in a thoughtful article in *Theology Today*,[2] rejects the activities of these innovators on account of what he calls their "mood molding" and "spineless aestheticism." Along with the superficiality of these liturgical revisions we may deplore a further unfortunate result, namely, the division of ministers of the same denomination into separate camps: the one maintaining stoutly that in the Reformed tradition, preaching is everything; while the other tending to temper any undue emphasis upon preaching and being happy to add more and more versicles and musical interludes to what they regard as a very thin diet of worship. Those who have friends or acquaintances in both groups know how subjective enthusiasm and "anythingarianism" marks the worship of one, while blasé professionalism and respectability are a façade for the other.

An editorial comment in the *Edinburgh Review* many years ago describes aptly the situation referred to above:

After the lapse of more than a century and a half, during which men seemed tolerably agreed to hold external forms of worship as belonging to the non-essentials of religion, and their rejection and adoption, consequently, as a question of expediency, we have had without any apparent cause . . . a revival of opinions more extreme than those either of Laud or the Covenanters. One class of persons we now daily see around us, approaching not only ritual forms, but even the most trivial and accidental usages of external worship, with an abject prostration of individual judgment which nothing could justify, short of a well-founded belief that they were indeed the institution of Christ himself. We have no lack of living examples of those, of whom Milton said in his time that "they cannot think any doubt resolved, or any doctrine confirmed, unless they run to that indigested heap and fry of authors which they call antiquity," and who conceive themselves as much bound by a well-authenticated custom of turning towards the altar when they mutter the creed, as by any article of faith which it contains. With such persons all power of distinguishing between the accidental and the necessary, the means and the end, is lost, and thus it is that the architectural arrangements of the church, its furniture, the dresses of the clergy, the order of the services (none of them indifferent matters when reasonably viewed), acquire a degree of importance which often seems scarcely consistent with mental sanity.

Opposed to these we have those with whom, in Laud's words, "a barn is as good as a church, and no church holy but that which is slovenly even to nastiness." In their case again the tendency is to repudiate, without scruple as without investigation, all the good and wise of former times have thought, said, or done, and to tread under foot the results of much learned and honest labor, as if to the institutions of Christian worship alone had been denied that progressive development which they themselves would regard it an extravagance to doubt with reference to any other. One party denies all power of judging to the present, and trusts for its guidance solely to the dim and colored light which shines through the painted windows of medieval tradition, whilst the other acts as if the opinions of mankind for more than a thousand years must necessarily have no other foundation than folly, or ignorance, or chance.[3]

This tension, moreover, is not new; nor is it merely a passing phenomenon. It is as old as the Church and its implications run rather deep. It is indicative of an ancient and perennial struggle between two seemingly incompatible opinions: preaching is merely a companion to a more elaborate and important rite; or the rite is merely a preliminary to the primary and central reality, namely, preaching. When these two positions are pushed to their extreme, we get what J. S. Whale called "the Protestant Word-Service" on the one hand, and "the Roman Catholic Mystery-Service" on the other. These extremes, however, are not our immediate problem. Our concern is more positive than merely to avoid the excesses of either school; it aims to secure *wholeness* in the act of Reformed worship so that services will not be one-man shows in which the personality in a central pulpit is the focus of adoration, even adulation; or that we do not become imprisoned by a verbal tradition which could so easily stifle or petrify the peculiar genius of the Reformed faith and the expression of it.

What then must be our approach to this matter of wholeness? Some people offer all too easy suggestions. They say, Let us go back to the customs of the primitive church. This is purely an over-simplification of the problem, because any such return involves at the outset a decision about the dates by which we bracket "primitive church." For, after all, the first two centuries of the Church's existence witnessed an evolutionary growth in the forms of Christian worship, and hence no one stage can be regarded as either a typical or final form. Indeed LeBrun maintains that no liturgy was committed to writing much before the fifth century, lest under the tyranny of persecution it might be used as evidence against the Christians.

Others say, Let us achieve a measure of conformity. Certainly this factor is involved, but conformity implies some approximation to a certain norm, and if this be neither delineated nor agreed upon, we are back where we started. Also, as George F. MacLeod has cautioned us, "A review of Presbyterian worship during the last four centuries would be sufficient to remind us that it never had a constant mode or form."[4] And then some others urge us to re-enact exactly what the Reformers did, without realizing that even in Geneva Calvin's wishes regarding worship could not be saved from contrary notions held by the Calvinists.

Further, it must be remembered that worship is a living thing, and the responsibilities and problems involved in its improvement are not taken care of completely by any ready-to-wear patterns of the sixteenth century. The problem of wholeness demands a more basic treatment. It requires first of all the setting aside of all secondary discussions about what items constitute a proper diet of worship and to concentrate instead upon its essential meaning. For when the meaning of worship is understood and formulated, we discover that it is related to a theological emphasis which determines the shape and supplies the reasons for all we say and do at eleven o'clock on Sunday morning.

Someone may contradict at this point and declare that in the Reformed tradition the place of preaching is settled; it has always been the primary factor, and that is all there is to say. It is true that traditionally preaching has occupied the central place in the worship of the Reformed faith, particularly in Scotland, and among the Puritans, from which the Reformed Churches in Canada, the United States, and other Anglo-Saxon countries have taken their origin. Indeed in many discussions of homiletics and worship the phrase "the primacy of preaching" is almost a household term. This is not surprising, however, because even in Geneva in early Reformation times it was customary to say ALLER AU SERMON with reference to church-going. Farel called his Genevan Liturgy: *La Manière que l'on observe en la prédication, quand le peuple est assemblé pour ouyr la parolle de Dieu.* And Calvin himself referred to worship as *fréquenter les sermons.*[5] Moreover, within Reformed circles to this day, it has not been uncommon to hear this remark, "I went to *hear* Dr. So-and-So at the First Church this morning." Such ideas, we grant, are faulty, even when suggested by the Reformers, yet we cannot blind ourselves to the fact that in the Reformed tradition there is a primacy of preaching that cannot be played down or abruptly dismissed. Now, by "primacy" we do not imply an exclusiveness by which all other parts of the act of worship are relegated to the category of "preliminaries"; but we do mean that both traditionally and currently, preaching has had, and does have, within the context of Reformed worship, a determinative rôle and influence. It must be kept in mind, however, that in these times of rapidly

increasing secularism it behooves us to emphasize strongly
the primacy of *worship* as "the Church's supreme activity,"[6]
yet we cannot close our eyes to the fact that in the Reformed
tradition a real case can be made for preaching as integral
and essential to its worship. Those who may question this
point of view must reckon with the following:

(a) Preaching was the foremost activity of the early apostles
and was instrumental in bringing the Church into being. "By
preaching," said Jeremy Taylor, "the apostles planted the
Church." Mark wrote about the work of the early disciples,
"They went forth and preached everywhere, the Lord work-
ing with them" (16:20). Perhaps no one has put the matter
more precisely than Dr. Farmer when he wrote, "From the
beginning, Christianity, being concerned with the Event which
by definition has no parallel . . . was committed to preaching, to proclamation. Whoso said Christianity, said preaching."[7] Also George Jackson remarked a generation ago, "It
was preaching that founded the Church, and it is preaching
which again and again, in its periods of flatness and failure,
has revived and restored it."

It is germane to this point to note that, in these days when
church expansion in America, for example, includes the organization of many new congregations in unchurched areas,
the initial thrust is always "a preaching service." No one would
dream of beginning a church in a new suburban area by setting
up a sign saying, "All Protestants are invited to a Communion
Service in the auditorium of the Kingswood School at 11:00
a.m. next Sunday." In such situations the role of preaching is
always primary. It is the actual spearhead or bringer-together,
while the Sacraments will give form and cohesion to the new
church later. They will symbolize the one-ness of the people
in Christ and provide the wherewithal that makes a church a
Church, rather than its being simply a group of well-satisfied
middle-class folk who meet together on Sunday morning. At
the same time preaching will continue as "obviously the basic,
pivotal thing without which other activities have little power."[8]

(b) Preaching is regarded as the most highly creative aspect
of the minister's office. In and through the work of Christ,
God's saving grace began a new and creative activity in human
history. The preacher whose message is a testimony to that
saving grace in his own life becomes part of God's great de-
sign for his creatures. He becomes a chosen man in God's
sovereign purpose. His studies, his prayers, his endless going
in and out as a cure of souls—all these become tributary to
the message he proclaims. These come into burning focus
during those twenty minutes when he tries to make plain his
personal knowledge of the unsearchable riches of Christ. Let
any minister flout the moral obligation inherent in preaching
and straightway the disintegration of his parish begins. That
obligation was put strongly by A. M. Fairbairn when he said
that the preacher should be "the man possessed of God who
speaks of the God who possesses him." This demonstrates the
preacher's spiritual creativity at its finest and only in proportion
to the price he pays for it will the fruits of his pastorate likely
be abundant, or even assured.

In his *Treatise on Preaching*, Humbert of Romans writing
early in the thirteenth century said, "Preaching is the foundation of the Church . . . according to Scripture; God sent
them (apostles) to preach, in order to establish his Church.
. . . The Church founded without preaching would not have
grown."[9] Centuries earlier Luke wrote in *The Acts*, "And with
many words did he (Peter) testify and exhort, saying, Save
yourselves from this untoward generation. Then they that
gladly received his word were baptized: and the same day
there were added unto them about three thousand souls"
(2:40, 41). After the great ecumenical gathering in Madras
in 1938, Dr. Farmer wrote, "Today, as the ecumenical conference brought home to us with irresistible force, the Christian
Church stands as the only truly international and dynami-
cally alive society in the midst of a humanity falling to pieces
around us . . . an underlying unity is there. . . . It is in a
large measure the direct result of preaching the Gospel."[10]

The Old Scots Confession of 1560 articulated the preacher's
responsibilities in this order: "The trew preaching of the
Worde," "the right administration of the Sacraments," and
"ecclesiastical discipline uprightlie ministered." The story of
the triumphs and revivals in the life of the Reformed churches
bears out the truth of Emil Brunner's remark that "the basic
or primal function of the Church is that of preaching: for it
is this which establishes the Church, in every sense of the
Word." And it is in the discharge of this high responsibility
that the conscientious preacher uses his material and spiritual
resources most creatively.

(c) Preaching provides the theme of the act of worship.
This may appear rather obvious and simple, but its importance
is seen within the context of the practical. Every Reformed
preacher will acknowledge that in the building and preparation of his Sunday services the theme of the sermon becomes
in certain ways the integrative factor. As we suggested earlier,
the order of service may, and indeed ought to be, shaped by
a dominant theological principle, but the selection of the content of this framework is determined largely by the subject
matter of the sermon. The hymns will follow a pattern with
provision for adoration, thanksgiving, fellowship, and maybe
dedication, but the final choices are influenced by what message the sermon is intended to proclaim. The Psalter and the
Lessons, if a Lectionary is not followed slavishly, are selected
either strictly in agreement with the sermon theme or as helps
to see its larger scriptural context. And lastly, apart from festival days, the organist or choir director feels that he can
prepare the musical program competently and satisfactorily
only if he knows the theme of the forthcoming sermon. In
relation to these practicalities, so very important in their execu-
tion, the preacher "declares the Word of God to give focus
to the various elements of the worship and to gather them up
round their center—the God who reigns and redeems."[11]

(d) The Reformers declared the Word to be the basis of
worship and faith. This was natural because in the Christian

life these three factors—Word, worship, faith—are inseparably
connected. All true worship presupposes revelation; this is
what distinguishes (or saves) it from being or becoming idolatry. Christian worship, moreover, is response to a particular
form of revelation, namely, God's Word proclaimed in Jesus
Christ; and the response is faith, the quality of which depends
upon and is molded by the Word that creates it. Now preaching is the initial way in which this Word is proclaimed to men.
And every ordinand of the Reformed Church is given authority
to do so as a minister "of the Word and Sacraments." Incidentally there is a sense in which this is not the most apt phrase,
because the Sacraments are not merely an appendage, but
are really the Word in action or made visible. The framers of
this statement might have said more appropriately, "a minister
of the Word through preaching and the Sacraments." Through
preaching the Word lays the claim of God's grace upon us and
it is up to us to respond in adoring faith and thanksgiving.
This Word will the true preacher, after hours of prayer and
exhaustive wrestling with it, proclaim before the congregation
with a note of personal joy. After he has done this, he will on
high and stated occasions bring out bread and wine and
through the medium of that ageless drama say, "This is my
body. . . . This is my blood." Yet this is not a separate act
or a different species of the proclamation of the Word. It is
preaching still. As John Bishop reminds us, "The Word spoken
and the Word acted are both sacramental, and it is the Word
which turns both the speech and the action into sacraments."[12]
And if the sermon has been Christ-centered, its implications
and demand will come to their focus and climax as the congregation responds in faith, "And here we offer and present
unto Thee, O Lord, ourselves, our souls and bodies, to be a
reasonable, holy, and living sacrifice unto Thee . . ." (*cf.
Book of Common Prayer:* Anglican; *Book of Common Worship:* Presbyterian, U.S.A.; *Book of Common Order:* Church
of Scotland and United Church of Canada).

From these discussions it can be seen that preaching is not

the actual equivalent or the whole of worship, nor at the same time can it ever be something done in isolation. Worship is the primary business of the Church and in that act preaching is in a prior position and should be shaped to direct and regulate all its parts.

To return now to our main purpose: What is the meaning of worship? Worship is what we say and what we do as a community of persons when we meet to hear in its burning reality what God has done for us in Jesus Christ; the thing we do and say being determined by our awareness of what we are and by the extent to which we have committed ourselves to him. Now every act done in the name or presence of God is properly a religious act, but it is worship only when it includes the proclamation of his Word and a conscious listening to him by a group of his people. In worship *Thou-and-I* is a relationship essential to it. It is the preacher's primary business to proclaim the Word of God's grace that came to its fullest demonstration on the Cross of Calvary. If preaching fails to do this, it has no place in worship at all. Preaching and worship at their best are always in a complementary relationship. Preaching declares God's saving activity to which the congregation responds in faith; hence for this encounter worship must provide the atmosphere and the medium in which the Word is most effectively heard and received. Daniel Jenkins puts it this way, "The preaching of the Word is a public act. It is addressed not only to the individual but to the Church as a body, and through the Church to the world on which Christ sets his claim."[13]

What then must be the character of the act of worship in which the Church engages and where preaching is done?

THE ACT OF WORSHIP MUST BE THEOLOGICALLY ORIENTED

At the core of the worship of every branch of the Christian Church there is a basic theological emphasis that gives shape and why-ness to the act. This is characteristic of the main denominational groups, but it cannot be generally applied to or regarded as true of the multiple sects of Protestantism, some of which are merely heretical aberrations. (Incidentally, the word "heresy" is to be interpreted here as the act of taking a portion of the truth and regarding it as the whole.) In the great Christian traditions this theological emphasis at the center of the act of worship appears as follows: In the Eastern Orthodox Church, it is the Incarnation and the whole subsequent drama of revelation in the life, death, and resurrection of Jesus Christ. In the Roman Catholic Church, it is Christ's death on Calvary, and in the service of the Mass the perpetual re-enactment of that supreme sacrifice supposedly takes place. In the Reformed Churches, it is the proclamation of God's will through the preaching of the Word and the Sacraments within the community or body of which Christ is the head. This central theological emphasis in each case authenticates what is done and gives shape to the liturgy that is used. (Some persons may protest against the use of the word "liturgy" in connection with the evangelical churches. But λειτουργία is a scriptural word which occurs six times as a substantive in the New Testament and is translated most frequently as "service," meaning simply what a congregation says and does in its act of worship. In this sense all the parts of an act of worship are liturgical, even the handshake at the close of the meeting of the Society of Friends.)

Now the shape or structure of a rightly ordered service of worship in a Reformed Church should conform to the implications of the theological emphasis behind it: the Word is proclaimed and the people respond to it by offering themselves in thanksgiving and obedience. Here worship and belief are closely linked. God's love is declared in the Person and Work of Jesus Christ, and the Church by its worship gives its reply through a pledge and covenant of faith. When this is kept in view the order of service can no longer remain a hodge-podge or *pot pourri* of miscellaneous items without any pattern, motive, or obvious rationale. It assumes a shape. And this shape, by its very nature, has a definite theological meaning. It consists of two major movements: God comes to his people in the proclamation of the Word and in turn they present themselves as an offering in acknowledgment of his claim.

The early Church moreover provides us with a precedent. As we saw earlier (Chapter 3) the records indicate that during the first century the Christians attended the synagogue on Saturday, the Jewish Sabbath, and on Sunday, the Supper or "the breaking of bread." Later, when they were forced out of the synagogue (circa A.D. 135) the acts of worship of both of these days became fused into the Service of the Word and the Fellowship of the Upper Room. And this continued as the framework of the formal worship of Western Christendom for the next 1500 years. Of course, through medieval influence the Roman Catholic Church acquired many pagan superstitions and embellishments which eventually the Reformers had to toss out, but the skeleton of the Mass was, and has remained, an actual copy of the early form practiced by the primitive Church. Calvin, for example, set out to restore the ancient simplicity. He had no intention of perpetuating the pagan accretions of the Mass, nor did he wish to create a *hiatus* between the Service of the Word and the Fellowship of the Upper Room. His desire was that "the acts of public worship should have due place for both, the Word being primary and the Lord's Supper—not the norm—but a normal part of worship without which the service would not be complete."[14]

The Act of Worship Must Be Psychologically Conditioned

When Reformed congregations assemble for worship on Sunday morning what occurs in each case is an action somewhere between two extremes: either abject passivity or unbridled enthusiasm. There is the type of service in which the congregation is merely a body of individual listeners; they are not involved in what is being said or done. The whole act of worship is performed by the minister and the choir, and evaluated incidentally according to their efficiency in "putting it across." This is an intellectualizing of worship in which the appeal is made primarily to the mind, without taking cognizance of the inclusiveness of the First Commandment which says, "Thou shalt love the Lord thy God with all thy soul, and with all thy strength" as well as "with all thy mind" (Luke 10:27). The other extreme becomes an exercise in sheer subjectivism. Most of the service consists of hymns with lilting rhythms and with words that focus upon the "me" in human nature; of prayers that are meandering introspective excursions; of pleasantries exchanged between pulpit and pew; and of smooth attempts to make everyone "feel good." In his classic liturgical work, *Le Culte*, R. Will passed judgment upon both of these extremes when he said, "Form without spirit is dead, but spirit without form is not capable of living."

These divergent types have presented caricatures of true worship because three essential things are either intentionally omitted or unwittingly overlooked: (a) in worship the whole man is involved; (b) in worship something is done; (c) in worship, what is done is always a corporate action. Regarding (a), the individual is not spiritually nourished, and certainly not redeemed, by simply clarifying his Biblical ideas or attempting to satisfy his intellectual wants. His feelings also must be influenced so that his emotions are cleansed, his aspirations channelled, and new and worthy sentiments formed. Just as the central theological emphasis gives shape to the act of worship, so can certain psychological factors save it from being an emotional bath, on the one hand, or an arid ministerial monologue on the other. As John A. Mackay put it in a characteristic epigram, "There must be order as well as ardor." Regarding (b), if worship is to have truth and spiritual actuality, there must be action in it. And, as we have pointed out earlier, this action is a climactic movement, consisting of the Word or the Event proclaimed, an encounter between the hearers and the Living God, and their giving themselves in response. Regarding (c), there must be a sense of community which knits or welds the various worshippers into a unit within the House of God. They become the Body of Christ. There can be no Christian worship if each person remains as an Alpine peak in the grandeur of isolation. Real worship is done along with others in a genuinely corporate sense. "It is made by a man with his brother in a beloved community."[15]

Now what are some of the chief psychological necessities that must be taken into account in order that the conditions of true worship may be fulfilled? There are at least four: objectivity, atmosphere, expectancy, and fellowship.

(a) *Objectivity:* Subjectivity has been the bane of much reformed worship and has made many of its services ineffective and maudlin. Such worship lacks a higher restraint to lift the worshippers out of themselves and a blazing vision to reveal to them a better existence beyond the level of themselves. P. T. Forsyth wrote, "Unless there is within us that which is above us, we shall soon yield to that which is around us."[16] There must be then an objectivity to worship. This can be provided and assured only if we begin to worship for God's glory and not our own. The focus of all Christian worship is a personal God who takes the initiative in the great spiritual act of re-creating men into the likeness of his blessed Son. Therefore, he, and he only, can be the focus of our adoration. Worship implies the priority of God, and consequently objectivity must be its keynote.[17]

This was the source of the depth and durability of Old Testament worship. It presented, as H. Wheeler Robinson said, "the objective worth of God as the ground of worship." And nowhere does it appear more dramatically than in Isaiah's moving experience in the Temple (6:1–8), to which reference was made in the Introduction. The initial vision is the majesty of God which angels and archangels acknowledge with the magnificent *Ter Sanctus.* The immediate environment becomes iridescent with an unearthly glory, and the prophet is moved to prostrate himself in the presence of the incomparable worth of Jehovah. He cannot presume "to trample his courts" because the place upon which he stands is holy ground. Then he cries,

"Woe is me! for I am undone; because I am a man of unclean lips, and I dwell in the midst of a people of unclean lips" (verse 5). The worship began with the unveiling of God before the worshipper, which in turn brought the unveiling of the worshipper to himself.

What a contrast between the objectivity of this approach and the vapid subjectivity of the initial act of many contemporary services of worship! Once a Presbyterian service was heard to begin with J. H. Gilmore's thoroughly subjective hymn, "He leadeth me," which was followed redundantly by a congregation-centered Invocation. Most Invocations, by the way, are wholly subjective and frequently read like a report of a committee on un-Reformed activities. The focus is inappropriately upon man, and not God, and therefore its appearance is generally untimely. The service should begin with a Call to Worship and a Hymn of Praise, followed by a strong Prayer of Adoration and a Prayer of Confession; in the latter the people will join with the minister. If there is a Processional, the Call to Worship may be given by the Minister from the back of the sanctuary. At the end of the Prelude the organist may play with full organ the first line of the Hymn of Praise which can be the congregation's cue to rise for the Call to Worship. After the hymn, and while the congregation is standing, the Prayer of Adoration is offered by the minister. It may take this or a similar form:

Lord God eternal, holy, almighty, merciful; maker of all things by Thy power, ruler of all things in Thy wisdom; we glorify Thee for the wonders of the heavens and the earth; for the perfection of Thy counsels; for the riches of Thy mercy toward the children of men; for Thy saving grace and truth revealed to the world in Jesus Christ; and for Thy presence vouchsafed to us through Thy Holy Spirit. All praise and adoration be given unto Thee, by day and night, with voice and heart, from generation to generation, O Father, Son, and Holy Spirit, God most blessed and most glorious, for ever and ever. Amen.[18]

Then follows the Prayer of Confession, which may be printed in the hymnbook or the bulletin, in which the congregation, seated and with bowed heads, joins in unison. This prayer should not be a catalogue of local ills and vices, nor like a Roman Catholic confessional, but should express deep and earnest acknowledgment of our state of sin and the moral fault within us that makes us what we are. It should be a cry for deliverance and may take this or a similar form:

Most merciful Father; we acknowledge and confess before Thee our many sins. We have transgressed Thy holy laws; we have neglected Thy Word and ordinances; we have walked in our own ways and fulfilled the desires of our own hearts. By our heedlessness and selfishness we have injured others, hurt our own souls, and grieved Thy Holy Spirit.

Most gracious God, who pardonest and absolvest all them that truly repent and believe Thy holy Gospel; show Thy mercy upon us, and for the sake of Thy beloved Son, our only Mediator, forgive us our offences. Increase in us the grace of true repentance, that we may not only confess and lament our sins, but forsake them with our whole heart, and bring forth the fruits of holiness and righteousness; through Jesus Christ our Lord. Amen.[19]

This type of liturgical movement will assure objectivity, without which the true meaning and focus of Christian worship cannot ever be initiated or guaranteed. As Oswald B. Milligan has commented, "We do not come to church to engage in exercises that are profitable to our souls, or to edify one another. We come to meet with God."[20]

Lo, God is here! Let us adore,
And own how dreadful is this place;
Let all within us feel His power,
And silent bow before His face;
Who knew His power, His grace who prove,
Serve Him with awe, with reverence love.[21]

(b) *Atmosphere:* Atmosphere in worship is created by a number of factors including the temper or mood of the congregation and especially the architectural form of the sanctuary. There are congregations, in the minority unfortunately, whose members come prepared for the service of worship.

Family prayers and cell-group meetings recall the various ministries of the congregation and undergird the health and prosperity of Christ's Church. The moments prior to the actual time the service begins are spent in quiet intercession for what is to be done rather than in a buzz of subdued whisperings or a round of millinery inspection. If, as the case usually is, the people come from the bustle of the secular world, it is all the more important that the sanctuary be made worshipful through silence or the creation of a mutual sense of reverence. "The Lord is in his holy temple; let all the earth keep silence before him." Or as R. S. Simpson has said, "There is an acquaintance with God that comes only through stillness."[22] To acquire this congregational habit may take years of subtle suggestion and steady education on the part of the minister, but its spiritual dividends will outlive his and many ministries afterwards.

Further, most churches have been built by laymen, or to be more exact, by committees, who had no sensitivity to the fact that there is a holiness of beauty as well as a beauty of holiness. Their barn-like structures have bequeathed to us ugly sanctuaries that have defied any rational or aesthetic explanation and have condemned succeeding generations to assume the burden of redesigning them. With the present expansion in new church building and the excesses of modern ecclesiastical architecture in mind, ministers of Reformed congregations should make their sanctuaries reflect the basic theological emphasis of their worship and they should use only those symbols that are appropriate to it. Architecturally there is no classic precedent to which to appeal or refer; certainly the Akron type is not the norm for Reformed Churches. If, however, the proclamation of the Word of God is central to the act of Reformed worship, then the best arrangement is a shallow apse with the lectern on the right, the pulpit on the left, and the Communion Table in the center. The lectern symbolizes the Word read; the pulpit, the Word explained or taught; and the Communion Table, the Word in action. There should be no objects on the Table—vases, pots, or empty collection

plates—for as a symbol it speaks for itself. Nor should the Table
be pushed against the wall to resemble an altar. Calvin pro-
tested, "We have no altar, because anyone who erects an altar
overturns the Cross of Christ where one sacrifice was made."
A bench for the clergy behind the Table and a Celtic Cross
on the reredos above it complete the simple symbolism.

Regarding the overall shape, a broad rather than a long
narrow nave is better suited for a Reformed service in which
preaching and hearing are important. Shallow transepts with
the apse form a compact entity and a gallery over the west
end of the nave provides for an ample narthex beneath. The
pulpit, table, and lectern will stand on the same level, a few
steps above the floor of the nave. They are not three separate
symbols but form a harmonious group that signify the proclamation of the Word through three facets. The lectern is one
of the oldest pieces of furniture in Christian worship and is
indeed a specifically Protestant symbol. And it is a most necessary object because the common practice of reading the Scripture Lessons from the pulpit is not Protestant, but Roman in
its significance. Whenever the priest reads the Bible in English,
he does so from the pulpit, thereby indicating that the Church,
i.e., the Roman Catholic Church, is the sole interpreter of the
Word. Also the central pulpit in Reformed Churches has allowed the preacher to dominate the service. He becomes the
focal point, not God. The result is that in many city churches,
to which we made reference in the Introduction, when the
"star preacher" is removed, the worshippers move also. On
the other hand, the pulpit must be imposing and spacious,
within proper proportions, and should always symbolize the
greatness of its function.

The choir is situated best in the gallery. To have the choir
facing the people "has no justification in history, doctrine,
psychology, or aesthetics."[23] This brings up the unfortunate
tendency in most American churches for the choir and its
director to become a professional order which vies with the
clergy for attention, prominence, and congregational prefer-

ment. In Reformed Churches *there is no such authoritative order as Ministers of Music.* The various Service Books have a ritual for Ordination to the Holy Ministry and those who are accepted for this responsibility and are set apart for it must qualify through certain educational standards, theological training, and evidence of adequate spiritual experience and resources. There is a varied ministry, such as Minister of Education, Minister of Evangelism, Minister of Visitation, but each of these in his own right is an ordained Minister of one of the Reformed Churches. Every minister welcomes good music and well rendered anthems as aids to worship, but the contemporary trend towards professionalism is alien to the original purpose for which choirs were organized and is fast discouraging the great institution of congregational singing. As P. T. Forsyth once observed, "To leave the singing to the choir and the praying to the minister is popish. . . . Originally the choir in Romanism was the clergy. They did the singing. They didn't lead; they monopolized. But in Protestantism, the congregation is the choir; the choir so-called is only the leader for use and service." No congregation should permit the choir to deputize for them. The Reformers brought congregational singing back into Christian worship and made it one of the marks of its corporateness.

To conclude this section, a passing reference must be made to symbolism. The ornamental is not necessarily an aid to worship, but symbols are, and they are employed even in the most simple liturgical acts. Symbols, however, are useless if they have no known meaning or if they are inappropriate theologically to the tradition in which we find our spiritual home. Rightly conceived, a symbol is not a representation, but a sign which suggests things too high or too deep for our human eyes to picture. If it enhances reverence and centers our befuddled minds upon God or his attributes, it is helpful to worship; if it calls attention to itself it encourages idolatry and should be removed. In the end, the acid test of all symbols is: Do they speak the truth in the name of Christ?

(c) *Expectancy:* Frequently some ministers attempt to attract the indifferent to worship through high pressure methods and under false pretenses. They create eager anticipation in the minds of those who have been vaguely interested, but the end result is inevitably failure. They should be concerned instead with creating real expectancy. This cannot be achieved through extraneous things. Something is required that is more spiritually basic than rousing hymns, instrumental solos, a brisk address, and coffee in the lounge for visitors and strangers. People should come to church with a higher expectation. As John Bishop has expressed it so well: "Throughout the service there should be the conviction that something is going to happen. . . . They are going to bring to God an offering, the offering of their praise and prayer in the communion of all his saints in heaven and on earth; and God is going to speak to them and have dealings with them, and receive their offering and give it a place in the service of his Kingdom. That spirit of expectancy is of the essence of worship in spirit and in truth."[24] And certainly this expectancy is more likely to be realized if, as was pointed out earlier, the congregation comes prepared.

Expectancy has to do also with need. Any congregation represents all the complex and hidden needs that our human nature is heir to. Broken and beleaguered personalities come to throw themselves upon the source of their spiritual help and sustenance. The service of worship must take into account all these varieties of moods and passions, particularly in the prayers, for there the subjectivity and objectivity of worship meet with real effect. The main themes of the prayers must include, therefore, Adoration, Confession, Thanksgiving, and Intercession, and in all these the minister who knows the human situation through the moral struggles of his people will seek to maintain proportion and balance so that all their wants are gathered up and no one goes away unmentioned and unfed. Such prayers demand unstinted preparation and disciplined devotion if the spiritual yearnings of all the people are to be met adequately. The lack of serious concern for the range and inclusiveness of the great themes of adoration, confession, thanksgiving, and intercession is the reason so many of our extempore prayers kill corporate worship.

What is more, and this is a paramount consideration, this expectancy in worship has a warrant. It is the product of Christian hope. And Christian hope differs from all worldly hope because it is founded upon the integrity of the promises of God. Christ has promised to be there to meet his worshipping people. "Where two or three are gathered together in my name, there am I in the midst of them" (Matt. 18:20). He is there in the preaching when the listener is morally judged and rejoices in seeing the way of salvation interpreted to him. He is there, above all, in the Holy Communion when as host he invites us to his Table. Not in any magical or superstitious sense does he come in the elements of bread and wine as the Roman Catholic Church would have us believe, but in the way Robert Bruce suggests:

You get a better grip of the same thing in the Sacrament than you got by the hearing of the Word. That same thing which you possess by the hearing of the Word, you now possess more fully. God has more room in your soul, through your receiving the Sacrament, than He could otherwise have by your hearing of the Word only. What then, you ask, is the new thing we get? We get Christ better than we did before. We get the thing which we had more fully, that is, with a surer apprehension than we had before. We get a better grip of Christ now, for by the Sacrament my faith is nourished, the bounds of my soul enlarged, and so where I had but a little grip of Christ before, now I get Him in my whole hand, and indeed the more my faith grows, the better grip I get of Christ Jesus. Thus the Sacrament is very necessary, if only for the reason that we get Christ better, and get a firmer grasp of Him by the Sacrament, than we could before.[25]

In this moment all God's promises come to their fruition. The action is the sign and seal of his finished work and is a foretaste of that heavenly Kingdom yet to be realized. What phenomenon could excite greater expectancy than that?

(d) *Fellowship:* Just as religion can never be a private af-
fair—although, as we said earlier, it can be intensely personal
—so with Christian worship: it must be social and corporate
in its expression. This corporateness is not merely "herd in-
stinct" or that emotional thickness that is created by revival-
istic campaigns. It is something quite different. It is a sense
of community. It is the highest fellowship. It is the living
Church.

Moreover, just as a Christian community cannot begin suddenly by fiat in a city or on a college campus, neither can it
be created by external pressures in the Church. As Harold
Roberts has reminded us, "Fellowship is found rather than
made. It is given as the result of a free response to a common
purpose."[26] In other words, fellowship is always a by-product.
Worship becomes fellowship when souls are united with other
souls by a common factor: Christ. "They are one body because
Christ is the spirit of each."[27] As Paul put it, they are ἐν Χριστῷ.
And when modern folk come together in this sense—all confessing a common belief in Jesus Christ as Lord and pledging
themselves to be his forever, his presence is more strikingly
and savingly real than on any other occasion. There is, further,
a contagious ardor in such fellowship whereby each is for all
and all are for Christ. They are ready for the sound of rushing
wind and the cloven tongues of flame.

This brings us to one of the most distinctive aspects of the
Church's fellowship in the Reformed tradition, namely, the
priesthood of all believers. Frequently this concept is grossly
misunderstood. But this need not be so, because clear definitions of it are not wanting. R. S. Simpson wrote, "In the Scottish tradition, the principle is clear: the whole congregation
is the priestly company making its offering to God."[28] This
cancels out such spurious notions that the priesthood of all
believers means that every man has a right to be his own
priest and to do those special duties for which the Church
has set the ministry apart, that an ordained clergy is superfluous, or that no one should wear a clerical collar. It does

mean that every Christian is part of a divine society; a member of the family of God. And with this comes particular responsibility. The clergy alone are not entrusted for professional reasons with the salvation of humanity. The entire membership of the Church must be the leaven in society and become the mediator in reconciling the race to God.

At this point, a brief reference must be made to the fellowship of praise, of hymn singing, in Reformed worship. Luther and Calvin were doughty pioneers in the matter of congregational singing because they realized undoubtedly that in this united act an emotional expression of the people can take place. The modern minister should be aware of this importance and give careful attention to the choice of hymns for the service of praise. The common temptation is to select hymns that are commended by their familiarity rather than by the standards of good theology, good poetry, or good music. When the minister caters to the ordinary level of congregational preference, hymn singing becomes an expression of their ordinary emotions rather than of their higher ones, the feelings and devotion they would own and express ideally. There must be therefore a lifting process in hymn singing that can be done only by virtue of the high quality of the words and melodies. It is greatly helpful for the congregation to sing

> Lord of all being, thron'd afar,
> Whose glory flames from sun and star.

It provides for them no spiritual benefit to sing

> I came to the garden alone
> While the dew was still on the roses.

The Act of Worship Must Be in Touch with Life

Any discussion of worship elicits sooner or later from the common man the awkward and troublesome question: So what? Most attempts to answer this query fall into the error of attributing to worship a definite utilitarianism and of suggesting that it can be used for some human end. But, as David

G. Peck, an Episcopal rector, has commented, "Worship is not a bottle of tonic which can be made to yield refreshment for any purpose."[29] Indeed, in the strictest sense, there is no such thing as *purpose* to worship. As we intimated earlier, there must be *meaning*, and in view of this, we cannot talk about the ends of worship but of those by-products that are realized though never specifically intended. The Shorter Catechism says, "Man's chief end is to glorify God, and to enjoy him forever." So is it with worship; it is for God's glory, and only insofar as it is so, will it have meaning.

Those who worship, however, are human beings whose lives are spent in a world of people and things. They live in an environment that is marked by a lack of reality, of meaningful structures and patterns, and of a clear sense of destiny. The majority are beset by a feeling of lostness because few know where they are or the *raison d'être* of their common existence. This unhappy condition has resulted largely from an inclination to divorce the material from the spiritual, the natural from the supernatural. It has come from modern man's repudiation of the sovereignty of God. Is it too much to claim that only through Christian worship will come that meaningfulness and order that men need so sorely? The ancient saint was sure that only in Christ's will can our peace be found. How then does worship bring together that holy will and the whole scheme of things in human society?

Suppose a worshipper, coming out of the frustrations of the workaday world where the accepted philosophies are "Everybody for himself," "This life is everything," and "Religion be damned," enters a Reformed church where he shares in a properly ordered and meaningful service. Through the opening acts of praise and adoration he is confronted with a Being other than himself, whose ways are higher and holier than his, and before whom he feels his own creatureliness to a disturbing degree. He joins with the congregation in a prayer of confession and feels a sense of self-identification with them as they ac-

knowledge their moral shame and impotence before God. With
them he says, "*Our* Father. . . . Thy *Kingdom* come . . . ,"
and by this he feels a gradual release from the tyranny of self.
In this community of persons he begins to realize that he can
never really be himself by himself. Then he hears the Word
read, and God's Will proclaimed and interpreted in the preaching, through which he experiences an inner encounter between
an eternal order and his own human disorder. Now he is beginning to see a glimmer of reality, but he cannot fully comprehend it because his rapport with invisible things is still weak
and tenuous.

Then the minister goes to the Communion Table where he
recalls in the great prayer of thanksgiving what Jesus Christ,
the Son of God, did for men and their salvation. He offers it as
one of the noblest prayers of Christendom, and then on behalf
of the whole community of worshippers assembled there, he
surrenders completely their souls and bodies to God and his
service. He takes bread and wine, and in the act of breaking
and pouring, he dramatizes the price and work of human redemption. The people partake of the elements, not only in
remembrance of what Christ once did or as seals confirming
the integrity of God's promise in the preached Word, but
signifying that they are receiving Christ into their lives in faith
and that he has become food for their needy souls. His presence in the Supper is an event of grace. He is at the center as
the one who died, but is now risen. As someone has said,
"Easter is there as well as the Cross."

The whole company then joins in a great song of thanksgiving to God for the wonders of his grace and to him alone they
ascribe honor, glory, dominion, and power, for ever.

As the worshipper leaves the church he sees himself in a new
relationship, the only relationship that gives meaning to life:
he sees himself as a child of God. And more, he sees the only
real pattern life can have and the means to achieve and maintain it. The service of worship was a recapitulation of Chris-

tian experience. The people entered as individuals, but they
came out as a fellowship of God's people, indebted to one
common Lord, and so unified by their spiritual experience that
no evil or disruptive force can ever put them down.

Worship then needs life, if it is not to be remote and consequently entirely unreal. The form of worship must provide
a pattern by which men can live in this ravelled and shapeless
society. That pattern is reflected in what is said and done.
What God has done to remedy human failure and moral helplessness, as recorded in Holy Scripture, must be proclaimed
with relevance to the common life and its promises demonstrated in the act of Holy Communion. Preaching then is essential. As Calvin wrote, "Without the Word the Sacrament
is but a dumb show; the Word must go before."[30] This is why
we preach. This is why the integrity of preaching must be preserved at all cost. And the longer people listen and the closer
they look, the more they grow into the likeness of what they
worship, and so eventually their lives become a true reflection
of God's Will. "To the Christian," wrote Maxwell, "all life is
worship. Not only at the Holy Table, but in his daily task he
offers his skill, thoughts, desires, and will to God." And the
contagion of this quality of life touches others, and these others
infect others, until the Christian community permeates society,
and under the aegis of the Living Christ remakes God's world.

6

The Order of
Worship

It would be a surprise, and indeed in some cases a shock, to point out to certain Reformed congregations that their act of worship consists usually of a jumble of religious items with little pattern or traditional structure on the whole. On the other hand it is equally disturbing for us to discover how many sincere worshippers there are who do not even care as long as the services are "bright" and the fellowship "warm," whatever these terms can mean. Yet if worship is to have meaning, a real effort must be made to realize in practice some of the Reformed principles suggested and framed in these earlier chapters. In this way alone will our worship escape the judgment passed upon it by a visitor from abroad who said:

People who would hiss a play which was so ill planned that the order of the acts and scenes was of no importance, or would throw into the wastebasket a novel which was so utterly without form that chapter 3 and chapter 16 are interchangeable, still pathetically

go to church on Sunday morning to take part in a disorderly medley
of music, hymn-singing, scripture reading, praying, and a sermon.
. . . Many church services today are a quaint mixture of concert,
lecture, and prayer meeting.

In order to appreciate the seriousness and truth of this in-
dictment, let us look at an Order of Worship chosen at random
from a collection of recent Sunday bulletins.

Organ Prelude:
  "How Brightly Shines the Morning Star"   Buxtehude
Doxology
Call to Worship
Prayer of Invocation
Hymn 192: "All Hail the Power of Jesus' Name"
New Testament Lesson: Luke 24:13–35
Anthem: "Worthy Art Thou, O Lord"   Willan
Summons to Prayer
Prayer of Confession (in unison)
Pastoral Prayer
Silent Prayer
The Lord's Prayer (in unison)
Offertory Sentence
Organ Interlude
Presentation of Tithes and Offerings
Anthem:
  "If Ye Love Me, Keep My Commandments"   Tallis
Old Testament Lesson: II Kings 22:1–23:3
Sermon: Is Your Bible Open?"
Hymn 216: "Break Thou the Bread of Life"   Bread of Life
Benediction
Organ Postlude: "Praeludium in C Minor"   Bach

What immediate impression is made by this order? Three
major, and indeed critical, weaknesses appear after merely a
cursory examination: no historical tradition is indicated or upheld; an absence of an inherent theological principle to give
it shape or form; no pattern that takes into account or approxi-

mates the psychological movements of the human soul. In
other words here is a service of worship consisting of a catalogue of items, each one commendable and respectable in itself, but when considered as a whole, making no liturgical
sense whatsoever. It lacks meaning. Its action is distorted. And
what is equally grievous, no participant would experience
more than a good feeling (never the end of any worship) from
having repeated a few religious lines, and certainly he would
not catch the startling vision of a new pattern for his existence
in the sense that all real worship and life are inseparable.

In the regular act of worship in a Reformed Church, there
should be three main movements: the Approach, the Liturgy
of the Word, and the Fellowship of Prayer. The shape would
appear as follows:

> *The Approach*
> > Organ Prelude
> > Call to Worship
> > The Sanctus (or Processional Hymn)
> > Prayer of Adoration
> > Prayer of Confession (in unison)
> > The Declaration of Pardon
> > Hymn of Praise
>
> *The Liturgy of the Word*
> > Old Testament Lesson
> > The Gloria Patri
> > New Testament Lesson
> > Hymn (or Anthem)
> > Prayer for Illumination
> > The Sermon
> > Ascription (or The Apostles' Creed)
>
> *The Fellowship of Prayer*
> > Offering and Dedication
> > > Anthem
> > Prayers of Thanksgiving and Intercession.
> > > Lord's Prayer.

Hymn
The Benediction
Silent Prayer
Organ Postlude

The general pattern of the above example of worship consists then of three parts: an approach and two main movements. The Approach is a period of preparation which helps to make the first main movement more exalted and worshipful. The Organ Prelude should be indicated and named in the service bulletin or calendar and be acknowledged as an integral part of the Approach. Indeed the ancient Scottish custom of bringing in the Bible by the sexton a few moments before the service is due to begin and placing it upon the lectern is an honorable and meaningful tradition and wherever feasible it should be adopted and encouraged. The Call to Worship, which takes the place of the bell in the Roman Catholic service, is intended to call the people to attend to the great matter at hand and it is effective only insofar as the minister himself hears it and responds inwardly to it. The words ought to vary from Sunday to Sunday and are more appropriate if they are meaningful selections from Scripture, particularly the Psalms. At this point sentimental poetry is as ineffective as it is banal.

Having risen for the Call to Worship the people will remain standing for the Sanctus or Processional Hymn and for the Prayer of Adoration. Since the Prayers of Adoration and Confession have been discussed already in the preceding chapter, undue time need not be spent on them at this stage, except to say that in the Adoration we become aware of who and what God is and in the Confession we express our consciousness of "our sinful nature, prone to evil and slothful in good." It might also be added here that towards the end of the Prayer of Adoration there should be some expression of the nature of an invocation that through God's influence the hearts of the people might see him more clearly and be led more meaningfully to the act of confession. This sentence would serve as a bridge of thought between these two prayers. From Calvin we get the suggestion that "after the general confession, some striking promise of Scripture should follow, whereby sinners might be raised to the hopes of pardon and reconciliation."[1] Hence the appropriateness at this point of an Assurance of Pardon which at its best is a declaration of the divine forgiving-ness of God. A Hymn of Praise concludes the Approach and is our response to God for his blessings of mercy and grace. The Psalter is a rich resource of selections for this purpose or suitable hymns such as Isaac Watts' "From all that dwell below the skies" or William Kethe's "All people that on earth do dwell." In this preparatory act we have recapitulated the real movement of the human soul. It is parallel to what St. Augustine meant when he said, "I was dragged up to Thee by Thy beauty, but dragged back again by my own weight."[2]

The first main movement is the Liturgy of the Word. Its meaning and significance lie in the fact that it "is the medita-tive, receptive rehearsal of the acts of God." It begins with the minister's voice announcing distinctly, "Let us hear the Word of God, as it is written in ———, the ——— chapter, at the ——— verse." At the end of the Lesson he may say, "The Lord bless to us the reading of his holy Word, and to his name be glory and praise." He must never say, "The Lord add his bless-ing. . . ." The Word is itself a blessing and needs no addition to make its mission or ministry more complete than it is. The congregation rises to sing the Gloria Patri. The New Testa-ment Lesson follows with its emphasis upon the work of God in Christ while the earlier Lesson from the Old Testament unveiled the nature of him who is the Creator of men and Sovereign of the moral law. Both Lessons should be selected with care, with the theme of the service in mind, with due recognition of the pattern of the Christian Year, and should never be merely the quick recurrence of the minister's favorite passages. The *motif* of the second Lesson is continued in a hymn that should be Christ- or Gospel-centered, although it need not be what is commonly known as a Gospel Hymn. The

Sermon comes next as an exposition of the Word which the
lections have declared. It should be preceded by a short Prayer
for Illumination. Here the minister assumes his prophetic office, but in his concern for the people and for the proclamation
of the truth he must not lose sight of the fact that preaching
is worship too (see Chapter 1). At the conclusion of the sermon
an Ascription may be given and/or the congregation may
affirm its faith in repeating the Apostles' Creed.

The second main movement, the Fellowship of Prayer, begins with the gathering of the offerings of the people. In ancient
times these consisted of gifts of bread and wine which were
placed by the deacons on the Holy Table and set apart for
sacred use. Today our monetary gifts symbolize the offering
of our lives, and therefore the service leads easily into the
Prayers of Thanksgiving and Intercession. Nor is the connection broken with the earlier proclamation of the Word, for
each hearer, as Robert Will wrote, "who opens his heart to
the revelation, will perceive his neighbor's faith inflamed along
with his own. The fire on each separate heart will unite with
all the others; till, like a single flame upon an invisible altar,
all this sacred ardor rises to God in one collective prayer."[3]
And the climax of the service is in the Prayer of Thanksgiving
just as in the Holy Communion it is the Eucharistic Prayer.
Arthur G. Reynolds put it clearly:

> It is surely a matter of supreme importance to us to realize that
> Sunday after Sunday, whether the bread and wine are present on
> the Lord's Table or not, full communion with God is open to us
> through this same prayer. Our history for the last four hundred
> years has taken away from us the weekly celebration of the Lord's
> Supper, but that is only to say that, if we will have it so, it has
> removed from our regular worship no more than the material
> elements.[4]

In the Directory of the *Book of Common Order* of the United
Church of Canada (Presbyterian, Methodist, and Congregational), the content or rather the shape of this prayer is made
clear:

Then shall follow Prayer, the minister in the name of all, giving praise and thanks to God for all his benefits, and above all for his inestimable love in the redemption of the world by our Saviour Jesus Christ; entreating God of his grace to receive the offering which we now make of ourselves, in union with him who loved us and gave himself for us; making intercession with the Father of mercies for the Church, the Nation, and for the whole family of Mankind, and for all sorts and conditions of men; and remembering with thanksgiving the whole company of the faithful dead who are now at one with him, especially those dear to our hearts. And then, Minister and People shall say together the Lord's Prayer.[5]

A Hymn of Praise follows, and while the people remain standing with bowed heads, the minister with uplifted hand as the ancient symbol of blessing, gives the Benediction. A few moments of Silent Prayer conclude the act of worship.

If the Sacrament of the Lord's Supper is observed, the minister will leave the pulpit at the conclusion of the Sermon and go to the Holy Table. The Service may follow prescribed liturgies in *The Book of Common Worship,* pp. 159–175 (The Board of Christian Education of the Presbyterian Church, U.S.A., Philadelphia, 1946); *A Book of Worship:* Congregational Christian, pp. 107–110 (Oxford University Press, 1948); *Liturgy* of the Reformed Church in America, pp. 29–47 (Board of Publications, New York, 1945); *The Book of Common Order:* United Church of Canada, pp. 110–139 (United Church Publishing House, Toronto, 1950); *The Book of Worship:* Methodist, pp. 369–389 (The Methodist Publishing House, 1945).

On examining the above Order of Worship, three factors may be seen to combine to give it this form: a theological principle, psychological movement, and historical tradition.

Earlier it was indicated that the revolution in doctrine at the time of the Reformation found its expression inevitably in radical changes in the act of worship of the churches involved. The key therefore to Reformed worship is the theological emphasis at the heart of it. As Evelyn Underhill stated it in a discussion of the character of the Genevan tradition: "The Word is the self-disclosure of the Eternal; and worship is man's

abject but adoring response to the utterance of God." God
speaks and man responds. The shape of the service becomes
the logical expression of these two movements: the Word revealed and proclaimed, and the human response in self-dedica-
tion. And the singular quality of the act is upheld by this
consistent aim—*Soli Deo Gloria.*

This service has a psychological movement also, which is
a counterpart of the central theological emphasis. God is
"Wholly Other." Man is a creature of earth and time. The
worshipper is made aware of God's holiness and of his own
unworthiness. Awe and wonder contribute to the sense of his
own helplessness. The original theological principle supplies
the main outline of the act of worship while psychological
considerations give acceleration, reality, and climax to its movement. As William D. Maxwell described it: "In such a service,
events come in their natural evangelical sequence. . . . First
comes the preparation in confession and praise, and then the
Word is read and preached; and so the way is open for the
great act of surrender and communion in the offering and the
Great Prayer, and if the elements be present, the participation
by faith of his Body and Blood."[6] And the Christian fellowship
is never more real, nor is a congregation more Christ's Church
than when it is led according to the appropriate movements
of the soul to this great moment of spiritual experience.

The shape of the act of worship therefore is basically a theological matter in the Reformed Churches, with many psychological factors arranging for beauty, movement, and a sense
of unity. But this is not the whole story, as we have seen already in Chapter 4. Our worship is embraced by an historical
tradition that is rich and significant in resources and meaning.
The Reformers attempted to get rid of medieval ceremonialism
which had made worship the plaything of a priestly caste and
to bring it back to the common people. What Principal Burleigh of New College, Edinburgh, said recently about the
Scottish Reformation was less provincial than he intended:
"The discovery of the congregation as the basic unit of Church
life and worship was, I believe, the great contribution of our

Reformation."[7] The Reformers' strategy was to recapture the early forms when the act of worship was infused with a first-hand relationship between the human soul and God and to restore their continuity with the Apostolic Church. Above all, they wanted reality in worship. The people must understand and mean what they are doing. And the deeper their comprehension the less necessary will be ceremonial and other paraphernalia.

But there has to be some sort of order. Moreover, it can not be so fixed that it is a kind of dead tradition that stifles creativity and the growth that results from fresh adaptations. Aberrations are the chief danger, and an historical tradition can serve as a corrective to them. The shape of the act of worship in Reformed Churches in America goes back to Diebold Schwarz in Strassburg who recaptured the ancient eucharist, stripped it of its pagan accretions, and passed it on to Bucer for further simplification. Out of Calvin's exile in Strassburg (1538–41) came his own adaptations of Schwarz's work, *La Forme* in 1542 and 1545. In Geneva he was prevented from celebrating the Lord's Supper, and the service became therefore the *missa catechumenorum* (or *missa sicca*), without the *missa fidelium*. The name of John Knox carries the shaping of our tradition a step further by his Geneva sojourn, but also through Valérand Pullain who fled from Strassburg with a Latin translation of Calvin's order and provided Knox's committee with a later edition (1554) when they compiled *Forme of Prayers* in 1555.

These, however, are the historical facts of our tradition, but there is a deeper and fuller side, namely, the passing on from generation to generation of the mighty acts of God in Christ from faith to faith under the judgment of Scripture and the creative power of the Holy Spirit. Our tradition then is a living one, because the Church continues to shape its worship in response to this revelation it receives.

Worship, to use a cliché, must be done "decently and in order" and, as John A. Mackay reminds us, "according to the

great proprieties." Here follow a number of practical suggestions; although they are rather miscellaneous in character
some ministers may find them to be helpful:

(a) In a properly arranged sanctuary, the act of worship
may be conducted by the minister from behind the Communion Table. Professor Doumergue assures us that Calvin
insisted upon this procedure. Maxwell agrees: "The Communion
Table has been the focal center of Christian worship from the
earliest times, and Calvin desired no change. With him . . .
The Lord's Table was the centre of devotion and fellowship;
and from it the worship was conducted."[8] To execute his
prophetic office he went to the pulpit, but at the Table he
offered in behalf of the Christian community the praises and
petitions of their hearts.

(b) Clerical dress in Reformed Churches is optional and
therefore wide ranges of selection and variety exist. There
are signs of a drift towards uniformity but there still remains
a haziness whenever an appeal is made to precedent or tradition. Nathaniel Micklem, in *Congregationalism and the Church
Catholic,* says, "The Congregational minister in his traditional
and proper dress, cassock and gown and bands, is not aping
the Roman priesthood but is the very symbol of the Reformed
religion" (page 59). Nolan B. Harmon, a Methodist, referring
to the hanging of the portrait of Francis Asbury at Cokes-
bury College, quoted from the record as follows: "Attired
in his long silk gown and with flowing bands the pioneer
Bishop of America took his position on the walls of the college."
The traditional articles of attire for Presbyterian clergymen
are gown, cassock, scarf, collar and bands, with the hood remaining optional. The story behind these includes a blending
of ecclesiastical and professional customs, but the main purpose has always been to efface the individual. The gown, in
use before the Reformation, crosses all denominational lines
and traditions and continues to receive wide acceptance. The
cassock, originally the "walking out" attire of all clergymen,
was common in the Middle Ages, but not until a seventeenth

century mandate given by James VI was it generally worn in England and Scotland. A portrait, for example, of Alexander Henderson, Moderator of Glasgow General Assembly, 1638, presents him in gown, cassock, and bands. Other portraits indicate intermittent use of the cassock during the eighteenth and nineteenth centuries. Its use is growing in this century, although thus far the hood, which is purely an academic symbol, appears more frequently.

The origin of the scarf or stole is not clear. Some say it is merely a remnant from a regular scarf used in ancient unheated churches. Others say—and this seems more probable—it symbolizes the yoke as a traditional sign of service. Ancient portraits and prints of Knox, Melville, Adair, and others, especially moderators, call attention to a somewhat general use of the scarf. In more recent years the ends have been marked by embroidered symbols (the Celtic Cross, for example); and the use of colored stoles, particularly by chaplains to the Armed Forces, has followed the custom of the Reformed Churches on the European Continent.

The bands come from medieval times and have been identified with both legal and ecclesiastical traditions. It is most likely that these originated from the "amice," an ancient linen cloth that covered the neck and shoulders of the priest. They have been in use in Scotland since the seventeenth century. Some say they symbolize the two tablets of the Law and are worn therefore by jurists and clergy to indicate their responsibility in dispensing or articulating justice. But the most common contemporary explanation is that they specify that the wearer is an ordained minister of a recognized congregation.

(c) The Sacrament of the Lord's Supper or Holy Communion is the crowning event in Reformed worship, yet few acts are more carelessly performed by a large section of our clergy. And this slovenliness is not always due to a lack of knowledge but chiefly of reverence. "Never in human story has there been less awe before the holy thing," declared the General Assembly of the Church of Scotland over a decade ago in its report, *God's Will for Our Time*. The Holy Communion is an occasion for dignity, based upon reverence, and is also a time when either the best or the worst in the celebrant can appear.

The Table ought to be drawn out sufficiently in order to allow freedom of movement for the minister, and especially to accentuate the symbolism of the congregation as a family gathered to partake of Christ's hospitality. At no time, moreover, ought the Communion Table in a Reformed Church to be pushed up against the wall, as we indicated earlier. The linens should be laundered with meticulous care and all utensils kept immaculately clean. During the Communion Hymn, and before the Consecration, it is better for the congregation to remain seated; this makes for less unrest and does permit the people to have an unobstructed view as the elders remove the cloth, the only remaining part of the striking symbolism which the Great Entry used to provide. If individual cups are used, a large chalice ought to stand in the center of the Table for the lifting of the cup at the appropriate time in the ceremonial. Also a slice of bread, about 2 by 3 inches, should rest upon the plate nearest the minister and be broken in full view of the people when he says, "The Lord Jesus took bread, and when he had blessed it, he broke it. . . ." The elders and officiating minister should discuss thoroughly beforehand each action and individual responsibility in order to avoid any embarrassing piece of bungling or disturbing mishap while the elements are being distributed. Further, it ought to be an agreed policy that during the Communion absolute quiet be maintained and all musical vagaries such as humming choirs and medley-bent organists be gently but firmly silenced.

The reverence that is demanded about the Communion Table belongs also to the whole sanctuary. The complete room has been dedicated and set apart for holy use. Sessions of local congregations must exercise more seriously their authority and responsibility in refusing to permit the sanctuary to be used for social entertainments, secular concerts, lectures and debates. On such occasions it is not unusual to find pulpit, table, and lectern shoved aside to become convenient repositories for hats and coats.

(d) Periodically a minister should examine objectively his own conduct of worship to find out whether or not some unconscious faults or sins of omission mar the effectiveness of his leadership and devotion. He may ask himself questions such as these:

(i) As I enter the sanctuary, am I prepared mentally and spiritually for the exacting assignment before me?

(ii) Is my conduct of worship a reflection of the great tradition of Christ's Church through the centuries, or am I a rabid independent relying upon my own peevish notions?

(iii) Am I free from all ostentation and oblivious to every distracting purpose except to glorify God?

(iv) Do I have sincere self-assurance or am I ill at ease, fidgety, and perennially flustered?

(v) Is there an orderly character to my act of worship, with minister, choir director, deacons, fulfilling their duties with clear understanding and rapport?

(vi) Is my service so organized that its beauty and strength come from its underlying unity?

(vii) Are my prayers fully prepared so that their appeal and substance are fresh and new and without hackneyed phrases and dull clichés?

(viii) Is my initiative so weak that I tolerate a forlorn and shabby sanctuary and thereby seemingly deny the existence of the holiness of beauty?

(ix) Do I, in following the main pattern of the Christian Year, make the program of worship more Biblical and instructive?

(x) Are my services sufficiently exciting spiritually to capture the immoral, to interest the indifferent, and to nourish the diligent?

(xi) As the service develops, do I become gradually less significant until the people see "Jesus only"?

7

The Worship Accent
in Preaching

MEDITATIONS

The Temptation of Worship

Mark 5:18, 19—"And when he was come into the ship, he that had been possessed with the devil prayed him that he might be with him. Howbeit Jesus suffered him not, but saith unto him, Go home to thy friends, and tell them how great things the Lord hath done for thee."

Wouldn't it be wonderful simply to remain in church all the time! To join in singing cheerful hymns of love and praise! To listen always to great choral music, the expressions of the flaming hearts of Bach, Handel, and Mendelssohn! How utterly fascinating it would be to remain within an arm's length of that untroubled world where everything is good and serene and where the sun doesn't go down and is never eclipsed by shade.

Or, to carry the idea further, wouldn't it have been grand to live in Jesus' day; to get to know him; to talk seriously with him on those long walks in the country or beside the lake and to feel the spiritual contagion of his glowing heart. That gracious pioneer in composing good children's hymns, Jemima Luke, was speaking for all of us when she said,

> I think when I read that sweet story of old,
> When Jesus was here among men,
> How he called little children as lambs to his fold:
> I would like to have been with him then.[1]

Now in order to be honest with ourselves, it is necessary to examine these deep-rooted desires of ours and to see whether or not our zeal to remain at worship is really genuine or is the wash of some ulterior motive. More frequently than we can imagine the real and indeed potent reason is that hard and ugly world that lies just outside the church's door. In Jesus' day, outside the immediate circle of his fellowship, there were harsh realities: the hated Roman rule, the quislings and traitors, the subtle graft and the character assassinations of an occupied country, the sickening lepers, and always the corroding poverty. In our day the story comes in another form. Outside the church there is a greedy world, where the fact that you are a Christian doesn't mean anything to some people at all, where conformity and compromise catch your idealism in a squeeze, and where you and I yearn to run back into the hallowed shelter of our Gothic fortress. For the disciples it would have been indeed a wonderful thing just to stay with Jesus. For us, wouldn't it be splendid to be able to linger indefinitely in church!

Actually this is what the man in our text was anxious to do. After years of fear, misery, and social rejection, this native of the City of Gadara encountered Jesus and was rescued from those mental delusions that were driving him insane. Now he was restored, and the fearful nights in the caves by the Lake of Galilee were over. Moreover he could resume his place in society and be presently and unconsciously a living example of what Christ does for every distressed person who has availed himself of his help. But this is exactly what he didn't want to do. He begged to be permitted to stay with Jesus, to remain within the shelter and security of the power that had made him whole. Then Jesus turned to him with the wisdom and firmness that marked so many of his decisions and said, "No! Go back to your home and your own people, and tell them all that the Lord has done for you."

This incident gives us in graphic form one of the most serious temptations of Christian worship: escapism. It is as old as mankind, but it seems to do the greatest harm when it seizes upon the followers of the Christian faith. Long ago it caught Peter on the Mount of Transfiguration—"poor, wobbly Peter," as Evelyn Underhill describes him—when he begged Jesus to remain there in some gilded tabernacle, far removed from the squalid crowd at the foot of the hill, with their aches and sores and tiresome wrangling. Jesus himself was sensitive to this temptation because it shadowed him all the way from his rendezvous with Satan in the wilderness to the lonely match with destiny in Gethsemane. Out of the struggles of his own life and the signal victories he had won he advised this new convert, "Go home to your friends and tell them how much the Lord has done for you." This was his antidote to the dangerous and hidden temptation to reduce Christianity to a prolonged act of mere hero-worship instead of letting it loose into the world through the personal witness of those who had been saved by grace.

The lesson is clear, and it reminds all of us that *the corollary of true worship is witness.* The Christian experience is never a matter of star-gazing. It means carrying on your habitual tasks, but doing so with a new attitude and sense of purpose. This is how the Christian faith has earned its peculiar character as a life to be lived, an experience to be made real in work and witness. These things, however, do not happen somehow *by* us; they are proof of the fact that something has happened *in* us. As E. Stanley Jones put it, "Something must happen to us before something happens through us." Now "a witness is someone who has heard or seen or known something; he has

a peculiar experience or piece of knowledge." But this something is not picked up on the golf course on Sunday morning
or at seventy-five miles an hour on the asphalt, regardless of
how fascinating the world of nature may appear to us. It
comes to us only in the worship of God's house and in the
company of his people. In the beginning it occurred occa-
sionally elsewhere—on some Damascus Road—but directly or
indirectly the church has been responsible ever since, because
it has kept this experience alive. It has been the channel of
God's grace. And whenever the Church has met to worship
its Lord in spirit and in truth and has recalled the deed done
once and for all for our salvation, some person has gone out
to witness to the great things he has wrought in us.

Yet every worshipper at some moment or other has been
dogged by the temptation to stay inside the Church. And this
desire has taken many different forms. Some have submerged
the living Christ in an ecclesiastical system and made order—
their order—an end in itself. "We've got him," they have
gloated; and as long as they have him as their exclusive pos-
session, no further witness appears to them to be either ex-
pedient or even desirable. Others have put him into a cell
and have drawn the shades of asceticism across every chink
and cranny, and in their stuffy solitariness they have felt safe
and warm. And some others have been filled with a vague
idealism and they have stood mesmerized before the old rugged
Cross, while the world of real problems and troubles stumbled
on its way. Like Peter they have cried, "It is good for us to be
here!" But all of these have a common fault: they have missed
the fact that the One with whom they have to do is the Christ
of every man. He must not be "cabin'd, cribb'd, confin'd, bound
in."[2] He is no man's private idol; he is not confined by eternal
decree to any one man's wave length. The early apostle said,
"We cannot but speak of the things we have seen and heard"
(Acts 4:20). And their tribe has increased until in countless
churches throughout the world each Sunday some worshipper
hears a voice, sees a deed, and is moved by the essential truth

of the Gospel to break out of the confines of both building and creed in order to tell his story to the nations.

We learn also from Jesus' command that *the fulfillment of worship is service*. Someone has said that the Christian life has both receptive and communicative aspects. This is true also of its worship. If the inspiration of the sanctuary is spiritually creative it must find its place of operation among the ever-increasing cases of human need. The temptation, of course, is to departmentalize the religious life. And the villain of the piece is selfishness. And whenever selfishness is allowed a hearing, our act of worship is truncated in quality and purpose. True worship, however, is bi-polar: it has to do not only with the worth of God, but also the worth of man. It is to God's glory, but that glory is increased and made plain in the redemption of mankind.

In worship we become conscious of God's will, but it is never to be separated from life. Worship is a means of grace, not an emotional bath for the congregation. It becomes then a sedative when ideally it should be a stimulus. Donald Baillie tells of a striking typographical error he once made. He had written the sentence, "The Church has a message," but mistakenly had typed an "a" for an "e" and discovered he had put down, "The Church has a massage." This is our temptation. We are apt to become deluded into thinking that the hour spent in church is the most expeditious time to bring our troubles to God and to receive a ready prescription for their cure. But this interpretation of worship dooms it from the start. To be meaningful, worship must be God-ward. Our eyes must be fixed upon One who is *the* Creator, *the* Power, and *the* Truth, before whom we are not anything, but through whom our pride and selfishness are broken and we grow into what we ought to be. In this way you and I share the life of God and it creates in us a passion to make it a reality in new lives and redeemed societies. This is the only service that is worthwhile. Francis G. Peabody wrote:

No mystic voices from the heavens above
Now satisfy the souls which Christ confess;
Their heavenly vision is in works of love,
A new age summons to new saintliness.
Before the uncloister'd shrine of human needs
And all unconscious of the worth or price,
They lay their fragrant gifts of gracious deeds
Upon the altar of self-sacrifice.

It is the quality of our worship that determines the dimensions of our service. As Evelyn Underhill said, "It really depends upon how wide we open our hearts."[3] And if men come to church simply as an escape, their presence in our common life will be the same afterwards as before. They will carry into life their old selves with all their egocentrism underwritten and intact. But if they worship God in wonder and in fear, the old idol of self will be dethroned and a new motivation will take hold: the desire to go out in the armor of God to do warfare against evil and to put forth hands of compassion to take care of the hurts of the world. For them, as Dr. Fosdick has said, "Christianity is not simply a message to be heard; it is a deed to be done."[4] Worship is fulfilled in service. But how we do and what we shall mean to men will depend upon how close we come to God in the worship of his Church.

Thanksgiving

Psalm 116:17—"I will offer to thee the sacrifice of thanksgiving, and will call upon the name of the Lord."

If you were to ask a representative congregation, "How many among you pray to God every day?" in all likelihood most of them would reply that they do so. On the other hand, if you were to ask, "How many give thanks to God?" it is probable that very few would respond at all. An older minister on retiring from the pulpit of one of the great churches of America said that the grace of gratitude was the most widespread sin of omission he felt in common life. Indeed Paul

included "unthankfulness" in a list of the worst evils of mankind (2 Tim. 3:1–3), while some others in a more positive
sense have singled out "thankfulness" as one of the best indica-
tions of the existence of true life within. Albert Schweitzer
called for this inner qualify of life so that each of us may
"become a spring at which men can quench their thirst for
gratitude."[5]

Whenever our lack of thankfulness is exposed or condemned,
you and I are very apt to become busy with countless frantic
efforts to remedy it. Some consider that maybe the passing of
a motion, "Resolved that we all should be thankful," would
change the situation speedily. Others feel that the whole matter
is taken care of adequately when a day is set aside annually
for national thanksgiving even though we do spend it selfishly
by feeding ourselves or grimly by our ever-increasing toll of
motor accidents. These efforts at thanksgiving, sincere as they
may appear to be, are not likely to amount to anything, because they are like outer plasters put upon sores that fester
within. We simply cannot experience real thanksgiving by talking glibly about it, or by a tip of the hat which common
decency demands we give to the source of all good things, or
even by long extempore prayers with every sentence prefaced
by a monotonous "We thank Thee, Lord. . . ." The demands
and implications of thanksgiving are far deeper than ordinary
secular conceptions of gratitude suggest. Indeed, only in the
Bible do we discover the real and proper nature of thanksgiving, where it is represented invariably as the counterpart of
a vital relationship with God. The Psalmist in the middle of
an eloquent song of gratitude gave us one of the finest pre-
scriptions for thanksgiving when he said, "I will offer to thee
the sacrifice of thanksgiving and will call upon the name of
the Lord."

Now, there are some among us who may criticize this declaration of the Psalmist by indicating that it appears to be a
jumbled text. Some others may go so far as to say that its
phrases must have been thrown together willy-nilly, or how
else could it have such a confused pattern. The Psalmist, they

say, talks about his offering to God but calls it a *sacrifice* of thanksgiving. Whoever thinks of thanksgiving as sacrifice? After all, sacrifices pinch and hurt while thanksgiving is associated with blessing rather than with pain. What is more, he labels the whole act as an offering to accompany his tribute to God. How can this idea be reconciled with the modern urge to go to worship primarily to relax and perchance to feel better?

These problems of interpretation cannot be solved until thanksgiving is loosened from any secular context where it can never be more than a private sense of satisfaction with the success of our own affairs. To be real thanksgiving must have a religious habitation where God's purpose in his creation is met with the gladsome response of man.

The first idea that becomes clear then is that genuine thanksgiving involves sacrifice. "I will offer unto thee the sacrifice of thanksgiving," sang the Hebrew poet. But his idea of sacrifice was greater than our simply doing without some enjoyment in order that another may have it. It was more than our merely going without chocolates or cigarettes during Lent as a pious gesture or an exercise in self-chastisement. This is self-denial with no positive end in view. A sacrifice of thanksgiving is entirely different. It is the joy we express to God when we see that everything we have given of ourselves has borne fruit in the pattern of his gracious purpose. This is the meaning of the words in Hebrews 12:2: "who for the joy that was set before him, endured the cross. . . ." Christian thanksgiving is an offering, but simultaneously it rejoices to see God at work among men in an effort to make them Christ-like. William Law puts it clearly in his *Serious Call to a Devout and Holy Life* (Chapter 15):

> Who is the greatest saint in the world? It is not he who prays and fasts most; it is not he who gives most alms, or is most eminent for temperance, chastity, and justice; but it is he who is always thankful to God, who wills everything that God willeth, who receives everything as an instance of God's goodness, and has a heart always ready to praise God for it.[6]

This kind of thanksgiving costs tremendously, but it brings a joyous satisfaction that cannot be duplicated elsewhere or realized by any other means. Karl Heim tells of an incident involving two children who broke through the ice near Stuttgart, Germany, some years ago. A passer-by threw off his coat, leapt into the water, and after much difficulty brought the two urchins to safety. "How can I thank you?" cried their mother. "How can I repay you?" "I don't want any reward," said the stranger. "It is enough that I have experienced this moment."[7]

The Psalmist goes further: he calls upon the name of the Lord. This is getting to the heart of worship. In the Biblical sense one's name was identified closely with character: Jacob meant supplanter; Ezekiel meant God strengthens; and Peter meant the rock. And in the case of God, naturally his name was the equivalent of his nature and character. To call upon his name, then, was to believe in his character and to accept his claims. It is therefore an act of faith. And worship, if it is genuine at all, increases faith both in quality and dimensions. "The worship of God," says Whitehead, "is not a rule of safety. It is an adventure of the spirit, a flight after the unattainable." Without worship, faith degenerates; in worship it operates and is made strong. This is why it is nonsense or rank presumption for you to say, "I can worship God on the golf course. I don't need to go to church." Has this kind of worship ever made a new man, or sent a Mary Slessor to Calibar, a Grenfell to Labrabor, or called five young men to martyrdom in the jungles of Peru? To call upon the name of the Lord is to respond to the claim of his spirit upon the complete potential of our life and character.

These are the things the Psalmist does. And he is glad in them because he sees beyond his sacrifice the realization of God's will for him. His faith in the outcome is strong, but not in any subjective sense. Its strength is based upon the immutable character of God. His experience had taught him what God is really like. "Death is vanquished, tears are dried, and fears are banished when the Lord is near."[8] God had never let him down. His heart was moved to love and praise God.

So it should be always in our worship. Thanksgiving is the indispensable note when we call upon the name of the Lord. But it is a sacrifice of thanksgiving. We praise God for what he has done for us in Christ, but our songs will ring hollow unless we pay the cost of the realization of his purpose in and through us. Ours cannot be less than "a living sacrifice." Our joy will be real when it is more.

Holy Communion

Psalm 149:4—"He shall beautify the meek with salvation."

If anyone were to inquire, "What are we doing here today?" the answer most nearly right would be that we are here primarily to thank God for our salvation. This, after all, is the motive and reason behind all true Christian worship. But it is not really as easy as all that, because someone from the outside—the quizzical fellow who always turns up—will ask the inevitable questions: What do you mean by salvation? Can you show me the difference Christianity creates between you and me? And none of us can rightfully blame him for speaking his mind, even in the form of embarrassing questions. Doubtless he has lost his way among the big names that mark the formal avenues of our faith and he is anxious to get a word of explanation from those who are "in the know."

"Salvation," writes Lesslie Newbigin,[9] "means the healing of that which is wounded, the mending of that which is broken, and the setting free of that which is bound." It is the revolutionary experience we have when we accept the adventure and liberation provided by the Christian Gospel. It heals our moral hurts, replaces brokenness with wholeness, and gives us liberty to aspire and grow towards our spiritual fulfillment in God's purpose. No man, however, has had the fullness of this experience poured into one single moment of existence; it is too great to be appropriated all at once. But usually he is able to witness to its reality as it is expressed through three tenses: past, present, and future.

The past tense of salvation is that crucial time of conversion when you reach a crossroads in life's pattern and you decide to give yourself over entirely to Jesus Christ. It is that high moment when you resolve to grasp what Christ has done and make it your own. For some it can be a sudden and almost cataclysmic experience like St. Paul's when a blinding light flashed into his eyes and a voice from the unseen upset his crusade of terror once and for all. It was like a great divide which created "a before and after" in the structure of his life.

For another it may be a gradual awakening like Henry Drummond's who described his turning to Christ like "the opening of a rose." Whatever the manner, the important point is that from this season forward, you and I are turned about and we have, as Leslie Weatherhead describes it, "a change of heart, a change of mind, a change of attitude, and a change of direction." Like Wesley's experience in the Aldersgate Mission we too might have sat

. . . where one was reading Luther's preface to the Epistle to the Romans. About a quarter before nine, while he was describing the change which God works in the heart through faith in Christ, I felt my heart strangely warmed. I felt I did trust in Christ, Christ alone for salvation: and an assurance was given me, that he had taken away *my* sins, even *mine*, and saved *me* from the law of sin and death.

The past tense of salvation properly takes no account of the manner or rate of conversion, but recalls the reality of the miracle that has taken place within the heart.

We live, however, in the here and now. Salvation has its present tense when it touches you and me within the flurry and fluster of the routine of daily living. Common casualties happen every day which indicate that men are fools to believe they can bear up by means of their own strength under the pressures of modern responsibilities or find their way by their own wisdom through a staggering series of clashing emotions and ideas. Men need salvation all along the line. And you have it as long as you are held and possessed by Someone greater than yourself in whom daily you give all your passion, zeal, and love. Paul put it clearly when he said, "I live, yet not I, but Christ dwelleth in me." And a twentieth century Christian, Helmut Gollwitzer, carried off to Russia as a German prisoner of war, with his hopes of freedom fading daily, wrote in his diary:

The great ideas have vanished . . . it is essential that I have somebody whom I love and who loves me. That is what gives meaning to my life and is therefore the ground of my happiness.[10]

There is more, however, to salvation. Its future tense is perfection. If Jesus had called us merely to be good, he need not have come at all; the Old Testament would be sufficient for us. But Christianity calls us to perfection: "Be ye therefore perfect even as your father in heaven is perfect" (Matt. 5:48). And Paul exhorts us to grow "unto the perfect man, unto the measure of the stature of the fullness of Christ" (Eph. 2:13). For some the goal may appear to be impossible, but each fresh vision of the Father's perfection in daily prayer and Sunday worship reveals new ideals to be pursued, new victories about to be won, and new heights to be scaled in his strength and for his eternal glory. Salvation then is a plan, God's plan, in three movements, described so clearly by Canon Guy Rogers, "We are saved *from* sin; we are saved *for* service; we are saved *into* the inheritance of the saints."

At this stage some pragmatic mind interrupts in order to bring our discussion down to his level and he asks, "What does this whole business of salvation really do for us? It seems so unreal in this hard world." Well, it does exactly what the Psalmist implies when he wrote, "He shall beautify the meek with salvation." Salvation makes people beautiful. Simple minds will laugh here because they can think only of those beauty treatments in TV commercials that promise a whole job from only a surface application. But salvation makes life

beautiful by giving it a new inner quality. And there is no
character more beautiful than that which Christ produces.
And you and I have seen in all walks of life human characters
reflecting that radiant beauty that Christ's saving work alone
can give. John Watson described Henry Drummond in this
way:

> One did not realize how commonplace and colorless other men
> were till they stood side by side with Drummond. Upon a platform
> of evangelists, or sitting among students in a dingy classroom, or
> standing in a crowd of passengers at a railway station, he suggested
> golden embroidery upon hodden gray. It was as if the prince of
> one's imagination had dropped in among common folk. He reduced
> us all to peasantry.[11]

This work, we said, is Christ's. But who are the folk who
are made beautiful in this way? The meek. "He shall beautify
the meek. . . ." Our modern interpretation of meekness, however, will scare any strong man away from the Gospel. Meekness suggests those soft, spineless, yes-men, who are always
compromising with the majority, and invariably to their moral
disadvantage. But there is something very wrong in this interpretation. Jesus said, "Blessed are the meek, for they shall
inherit the earth." Surely then the meek are among the in-
vincible. Dr. Ralph Sockman has pointed out that in the Old
Testament the original meaning of the word for "meek" suggested "those who are being moulded." And this spiritual
fashioning is done by God.[12] The meek are those who are willing to forget themselves and literally submerge themselves
in Christ's cause and for Christ's purpose. The meek are the
adaptable folk who accept life as it is, who fit themselves into
it, but at the same time they never sacrifice nor compromise
their moral principles. They are not described anywhere more
plainly than in the invitation to the Sacrament of the Lord's
Supper in *The Book of Common Worship:*

> All that humbly put their trust in Christ, and desire his help
> that they may lead a holy life, all that are truly sorry for their
> sins and would be delivered from the burden of them, are invited
> and encouraged in his name to come to this Sacrament.[13]

And when the meek come to the Lord's Table to handle and partake of the sacred symbols, they do so in a spirit of repentance and humility and are prepared then to renew their costly allegiance to Christ. They realize also that when they come in this mood they cannot go away and be the same again. They are touched by a beauty which the grime of common life cannot deface. And it is the beauty of salvation. Horatius Bonar must have seen the meek in companies around the Table when he wrote the lines of one of the classics among Communion hymns:

> I have no help but thine; nor do I need
> Another arm save thine to lean upon;
> It is enough, my Lord, enough indeed;
> My strength is in thy might, thy might alone.
>
> Mine is the sin, but thine the righteousness;
> Mine is the guilt, but thine the cleansing blood;
> Here is my robe, my refuge, and my place—
> Thy blood, thy righteousness, O Lord my God.
>
> Feast after feast thus comes and passes by,
> Yet, passing, points to the glad feast above,
> Giving sweet foretaste of the festal joy,
> The Lamb's great bridal feast of bliss and love.[14]

Easter

Rev. 1:18—"I am he that liveth, and was dead; and, behold, I am alive for evermore."

John 14:19—"Because I live, ye shall live also."

> There we shall with thee remain
> Partners of thy endless reign.

So wrote Charles Wesley about one of the many benefits of the Resurrection. But how many persons who throng our churches at this season are apt to make this thought the total message of Easter Day! Most of them think that the primary meaning of Easter is that they will live forever, and that somehow they are automatically the heirs of Jesus' valedictory claim for his disciples, "Because I live, ye shall live also." Indeed not a few of those who seem to feel that worship is obligatory only on Easter Day are apt to consider their attendance the equivalent of free transportation to the land of endless day.

How easily do these people miss the primary meaning of the Resurrection. Jesus' followers were glad on Easter morning, but it was not from being suddenly informed or convinced that they were to live forever. It is doubtful if this notion ever occurred to them. They were glad because *Jesus was still alive.* As John wrote, "Then were the disciples glad when they saw the Lord" (Chap. 20:20). Without this triumphant fact, these folk would have known the same sad implications suggested by Mephistopheles' remark to Faust: "The ultimate value of everything is nothing."

Easter has never been a simple endorsement or promise of your immortality or mine. The central fact proclaimed on that third day was that Christ was alive, that all he was and all he stood for had vanquished the Cross. But most Easter worshippers like to forget the Cross; they find it to be all too disturbing; and this is their reason for trying to smother its grim form with blooming flowers. "The three sad days have quickly sped," so they sing; and they try to forget the tears of Gethsemane and the pain of Good Friday by decorating them with the ornaments of immortality. But Easter does not somehow write off Good Friday. It confirms and vindicates it. And any attempt to cancel out the Cross from Easter Day is to produce a cult of sheer sentimentality.

Unfortunately this cult has practically taken over the real significance of the Resurrection and as a result people come to worship on Easter Day with the impudent idea that they are not expected to be serious about it anyway. With almost a cavalier mood they dismiss the Cross for the idols of the florist and milliner's trade. Is not the time ripe for us to confront these flitting Easter worshippers with the reproach that no man has any right to Easter who has not been with his Master through Good Friday?

Eternal life is the greatest blessing Easter brings and, according to the Reformed tradition, it is a gift of God's grace. It hasn't anything to do with length of time, but it is a quality of life which God alone can give. Yet there is a sense in which it is also earned by those who realize and possess it. None of us could really appreciate this quality of life unless first we had gone through the process of losing our life in order to find it. Easter teaches us that real life—eternal life—is a by-product of a spiritual partnership with the Son of God. And the joy that was his can be ours too if we do not attempt or presume to by-pass or eliminate the Cross. "It is not the act of a good disciple," said St. John of the Cross, "to flee from the Cross in order to enjoy the sweetness of an easy piety." We must pass through the Cross if we are to share the life of God. Hence the truest symbol of our faith is a Cross encircled with a Crown. Only a shallow Christian would conclude that his annual salute to Easter Day is a passport to eternal life. Paul Scherer made it plain with characteristic forcefulness: "The Cross is the only strategy God will underwrite." And when genuine believers accept this fact and proceed by "the way of the Cross" they have taken the first long step towards life's greatest triumph. They know this is God's way and they are aware of the Good News that the Lord of Life has gone ahead of them and covered the Cross with the blazing light of his royal victory.

Our Easter worship then must be rid of all mawkish sentimentality. It must declare that Christianity is stern business when compared with what is suggested by lilies, rabbits, and colored eggs. It must proclaim that a man died rather than go back upon his Father's will and because his love for men would not allow him to do otherwise. This is the fact behind Easter, and for this reason our fashion parades are like rattling and raucous noises in the presence of the pure music of heaven. Only the sincerest worship can be associated with the name of Easter. And the values of that worship will never be fully realized unless all of us come to Easter Day by way of the hill called Calvary. Then we shall have seen sin at its worst, love at its highest, and God's power mightily at work.

> "Welcome, happy morning!" age to age shall say:
> "Hell today is vanquished, heaven is won today."
> Lo! the dead is living, God for evermore:
> Him, their true Creator, all His works adore.[15]

SERMONS

Before Worship: Preparation

Topic: "Are You Ready for Church?"

Text: Psalm 24:3–5.

William Barclay tells us about a party of tourists who were visiting Germany in the early 'thirties and were being shown the actual room in which Beethoven had lived and worked. In one corner stood an old piano which was reputed to be the very instrument on which he had composed the famous *Moonlight Sonata*. One of the tourists—an American girl—rushed to the piano and thumped out the first movement of the sonata. When she finished and returned to the group with an air of juvenile triumph, the guide remarked, "You will be interested to know that we had Paderewski himself as a visitor here last week." "Really?" replied the girl, "and I bet he did just what I did. I'll bet he sat down and played the sonata!" "No, Miss," said the guide, "he didn't. Everyone begged him to do it, but he said, 'No, no! I am not worthy.'"

Men and women, how carefully did you prepare yourself for church today? Most of us can appreciate the fact that you were quite meticulous about the condition of your clothes and whether the colors were matched, and perhaps you attended faithfully to all the routine matters of the household; but how many of you thought there was anything else in need of preparation? The body? Yes! The time schedule? Of course! But what about the heart, or the soul, or the mind?

This brings the matter painfully close to all of us. How many persons ever think of preparing themselves spiritually for the exercises of God's house at eleven o'clock on Sunday morning? Or to how many does the idea of worthiness ever occur? Some preachers focus their attention upon the absentees and scold them for the trivial reasons that have kept them away, but all this can be merely wasted effort, for obviously these delinquents are safely beyond the range of any word of condemnation from the pulpit. Our question therefore is more pertinent, and for this reason all the more disturbing and startling, because it has to do with those who are present. It confronts you and me with questions such as these: Who prepared himself to come to church today? Who has the right to come? Who is actually worthy to tread these sacred courts?

This is the impressive note that is sounded in the Twenty-fourth Psalm. The occasion was one of those truly great days in the history of the Hebrew people, a time in which their worship was celebrated in grand style. Tradition has it that the Ark of God, the symbol of Jehovah's presence with his people, was being carried with triumphant shouts up the hillside to be set in the Temple. And we can almost see the nation coming from near and far and forming a chanting processional behind the slowly moving carts. But as the gates are lifted and the flourish of trumpets heralds the arrival of the Ark, a question jolts these people almost to a halt: "Who dares to approach the hill of the Lord? Who is worthy to enter the portals of Zion?" Only those whose hands are clean and whose hearts are pure are entitled to come in, but a barrier rises before those who "have lifted up their souls unto vanity" or "sworn deceitfully." They were not to be accorded the blessings of the worship of the sanctuary. They were not, however, heinous sinners, but could be easily you or I who enter with careless informality or trample this sacred place where God's honor dwells and where, confronted by the purity of his holy Being, we are exposed for what we are.

But someone interrupts and charges that if you exclude the

man who has "lifted up his soul unto vanity," you will have
barred the sinner from church. And is it not the church's
primary business to try to bring every sinner under the blessing
of its worship? Yes, that is true; the church does keep an
ever-open door for sinners, but they must be sinners of a
certain kind: they must be sinners who yearn to be made whole.
The man who has "lifted up his soul unto vanity," however,
is a very different type, and rather a shameful one at that.
He comes to church on Sunday, but at the same time his heart
and mind are set upon everything that is inimical or opposed
to God. What is transitory and unreal has priority over his
Father in Heaven every time. The god he really worships is
his business or investments, and at no time in the act of worship is he anything more than a detached spectator. He is shot
through with a smug self-satisfaction which defies the possibility of anything happening anyway. This man, the Psalmist
considers, is unworthy to come to church, because he simply
will not identify himself with those confessing and surren-
dered souls to whom the very stones of God's House are dear.

But he is not alone. The man who has "sworn deceitfully"
is not ready either. But surely, you say, he is not one of us.
Just a moment! What does it mean to swear deceitfully?
Mainly it is to give your allegiance or to measure your behavior
by what you know to be untrue. It is to live your life from
Monday to Saturday according to standards that contradict
what God has written into the moral nature of his universe.
Such a person is not worthy to enter the gates of God's House
because he persists in living a lie in his heart. Indeed any man
who tries to worship according to the law of Christ on Sunday
and to run his business all week by the law of the jungle actually contradicts, annuls, and negates what the church is and
all it stands for in the world.

Who then dares to ascend the hill of the Lord? And who
is worthy to stand in his holy place? You see the question that
faces you and me every Sunday morning is basically: Am I
ready for church? Clean hands and a pure heart are not so
much conditions to worship as they are marks of an inner

disposition or state of being that makes real worship possible. It is the mood of him who has tried to do right but who throws himself finally upon God and asks for pardon for doing what he ought not to have done and leaving undone what he ought to have done. In his helplessness he comes to the source of all help and reaches out for the hand of everlasting mercy. Up to the best of his ability he has tried to do the right by his fellowman before bringing his gift to the altar. For him, outside the church are the tyranny of routine, the canker of moral compromise, and the slow cramping of all genuine aspiration, and so he comes into the sanctuary to be captured by a new spiritual adventure under God and to be one in faith and fellowship with those whose aims and ends are good.

It is clear now that preparation for church has to do with a sense of purpose in the worship in which you and I engage. There are devotional exercises that are particularly helpful in shaping our attitudes and temperament for worship, but beyond these we must possess the right intention that will prepare us to receive the blessing God has promised to provide.

First of all, you are ready for church *when you come not to get, but to give.*

Have you ever listened to the reasons some people give for staying away from church? One man declaims with a surge of righteous indignation, "That church of ours is full of draughts; I get a cold every time I go!" Yet in all likelihood he'll stand in a line-up at a movie theatre for a whole hour on a frosty night. Another says with a shrug of impatience, "I don't get anything out of that young man's sermons; I stopped going when Dr. So-and-So left!" Unfortunately in this case the church is identified with the preacher and the reputation of the former is dependent solely upon the latter. Or another says, "I don't go myself, but I see to it that the children always go." What will these children think or do, however, in years to come? Remember the little girl who asked her mother, who was indifferent to religion, "When shall I be old enough to stop saying my prayers?"

All these people are so terribly wrong in their conception of what the purpose of worship is in the sanctuary on Sunday morning. It can never be a matter of saying that the church has nothing to interest me and therefore I will not attend. But what about those who do come? Is it clear to their minds that worship consists not in getting but in giving? One of the most dangerous heresies abroad in American Protestantism today is that you go to church *to get something*—peace of mind, relaxation, and the like. If you come to worship with nothing more than a hang-over from a dissipated week and with an offering that is a meagre left-over after every human whim is satisfied and with the narrow expectation that somehow it will pay off, then you will go away empty and dissatisfied, at odds with both God and man. Emil Brunner once said that in worship "the decisive thing is whether you are offering yourself to God."[16] And those who cry that they have gotten "nothing out of the service" can account for it invariably by the fact that they put nothing into it. They make no offering to God, but simply try to use him for the satisfaction of their own social or pecuniary needs.

True worship, on the other hand, means fellowship. No man has ever had a private god. And Christian worship, more emphatically than all others, is done by the corporate group to which each brings something of himself. No one therefore can come to church with his mind made up to sit in solitariness. Indeed C. Anderson Scott indicates that "fellowship was the earliest self-designation which the Christian community adopted." You cannot be alone in worship. You must be prepared to give to the whole, and in this way only you will be able to move away from self. This is not to think, however, that the congregation is simply a jolly group bound together by a warm feeling. "The Christian fellowship," says H. F. Lovell Cocks,[17] "has no life in itself. It lives only as it shares the eternal life of God." Only as you and I give ourselves earnestly to God in response to what he has done for us will we realize in our worship that fellowship which can repair our common life and is a pledge of his everlasting kingdom.

Then, second, you are ready for church *when you come not to enjoy yourself but to share in something that is done.*

One day at the close of a service, a woman said to Phillips Brooks, "I enjoyed your sermon very much." With an impressive sense of finality the great New England preacher replied, "Madam, it wasn't meant to be enjoyed."

Here, in a half-dozen words, he struck at one of the most serious and most prevalent misconceptions of the nature of worship held by even some of our best church-goers today. The fault runs deep. And its outward characteristics appear in some of those popular religious habits that ordinarily we commend but in our more thoughtful moments we deplore. To far too many people the minister and choir are performers engaged in a show which they must "put across" and therefore these "would-be" worshipers hurry in criss-cross fashion all over our larger cities to seek out some church where the preacher or choir has a reputation for "pulling them in." For them worship never goes beyond being something to be enjoyed, as any other secular program might be. This can never be less than an outrage against the Christian idea of a church as a community of believers met to adore God through whose redemptive work they have found the highest life.

Someone among you may ask at this point about the matter of beauty in worship. Its place must be kept inviolate, because as James A. Pike has said, "In worship we place ourselves in a specialized atmosphere in which the most wholesome things can reach us."[18] Here rests any plea for the aesthetic in worship, but at the same time it must not be an end in itself and therefore become idolatry. This would be lifting our souls unto vanity. Beauty is meant to help us in the thing that is being done—namely to worship God. It goes hand in hand with symbolism which has always had a traditional rôle in worship, but it degenerates and runs into peril when it becomes an end in itself or is identified completely with the object of worship itself as in pagan and Roman Catholic rituals.

Now what is this thing that is done in worship in which all

of us must share? For some people the temptation merely to
enjoy themselves can be very real because it is related so
closely to that subjective something they feel. But something
is done, which David Hislop defined in this way: "Communion
with God is the laying of our wills beneath God's will." When
we worship God as the Creator and Redeemer of men there
is laid upon us the claim of his will, and if he is what we
adoringly say he is, then what are we to do about it? "O magnify the Lord with me," said the Psalmist. And here "magnify"
means "to make great." This is what we do—we make God
great in our lives. And to make him great is to accept him as
the source and center of all truth. And since you and I always
become like what we worship, we shall assimilate a part of
truth in these exalted hours. This truth, however, is not a
proposition; it is personal. Moreover, it is living and creative
because it is God's truth. Worship is something you do, not
in the sense that it is a matter of kneeling or singing or reciting
a creed, necessary as these are; but it is an acknowledgment
by a company of kindred believers that here alone is the secret
of life; here is its meaning most clearly seen. Here is salvation,
for here is truth alive in God's act, the giving of his Son. By
this we are claimed; to this we surrender; in this we find the
highest thing we can ever do.

Third, you are ready for church *when you come not to
perpetuate what you are, but to realize what you can become.*

Last summer I re-read Charles M. Sheldon's once famous
book, *In His Steps,* which in its day sold over a million copies
and which, I imagine, many of our older people have read.
The dramatic story revolved around the First Church in the
city of Raymond, which had—to quote the author—"the best
choir . . . a membership composed of the leading people, representative of the wealth, society, and intelligence of the city . . .
a church which congratulated itself on having in its pulpit so
scholarly and refined a minister as Dr. Henry Maxwell." Suddenly one beautiful Sunday morning, into the midst of this
congregation of self-adulators, there was precipitated a star-

tling and embarrassing incident when, after the soloist had sung so feelingly "Where He Leads Me I Will Follow," there shuffled down the aisle a dirty, shabby-looking tramp, who turned to these self-confident people and asked, "What do you mean when you sing 'I'll go with him, with him, all the way?" And some of you will remember how out of this situation there came a spiritual revival that shook one city after another and sent men of influence and power into the service of Christ.

Worship can be a deadening experience when we come to it firmly set in our own opinions and aspiring towards nothing beyond and above ourselves. Bliss Carmen, the Canadian poet, caught our failure in these lines:

> They're praising God on Sunday.
> They'll be all right on Monday.
> It's just a little habit they've acquired.[19]

And a bit of doggerel verse is not without its point:

> Like a mighty tortoise
> Moves the Church of God.
> Brothers, we are treading
> Where we've always trod.[20]

Lovell H. Cocks speaks of churches which "have not so much as heard of the Holy Spirit, or, if they have heard of him they will admit him only on condition that he changes nothing and disturbs nobody."[21] And Dr. Fosdick deplores those worshipers who "come from church with all their bigotries, sharpened and confirmed."[22]

All these have one ailment in common: they come to church in search of some divine endorsement of what they already are and without any genuine intention of allying themselves with that Power that alone can lift them out of themselves and make them something better than themselves. They are not prepared "to let go and let God," because they fear the consequence of what Paul Scherer suggested when he said, "Nothing is safe in this world with a living God around." Noth-

ing is safe—your shallow respectability, your pride in mere
goodness, your fondness for the *status quo*—none of these is
safe once you have come to church resolved to take God
seriously. Even your destiny can be at stake. And the Wesleys,
Spurgeons, and Grenfells of history are witnesses to this incontrovertible fact.

It becomes obvious then that to be ready for church is
basically a matter of faith. You come in faith and you meet
an experience of grace. To give yourself to God in the fellowship of the church or to surrender your will to the claim of his
purpose is a tremendous overture of faith. And it takes real,
costly faith on your part and mine. In this experience the old
patterns and structures of our common life are broken up and
we become big with promise, great in our Christian destiny,
and worthy to receive the blessing which fellowship with the
Unseen supplies.

Are you ready for church? You are if you come with eye,
ear, and heart centered on him, without whom no worship is
either real or even possible. As Pascal declared more than three
centuries ago to a great congregation in Paris, "I see him in
all his splendor . . . and lo! he is on his way to God. But
now—I see him turn, and now I see him smile and cry: 'I am
the Way, the Truth, and the Life. O, France, follow me, and
win the Crown.' "[23]

After Worship: Consecration

Topic: "For Their Sakes"

Text: John 17:19 (Moffatt)

When you sing the well-known hymn

> Take my life, and let it be
> Consecrated, Lord, to Thee.

do you ever pause long enough to realize how great is the
risk you are assuming? Verse by verse you offer some of your
capacities or powers to God's exclusive use, until in the final
stanza you sing

> Take myself, and I will be
> Ever, only, all for thee.

It is obvious that no one of us can sing this hymn honestly and sincerely and ever presume to be the same again. Here indeed is the yardstick that measures the dimensions of your consecration. Here you are reminded of how much you are ready and willing to give to God and how jealously and selfishly you hold some other things back.

Ian MacPherson[24] tells us that one day Philip de Neri, the sixteenth century Italian mystic, was crossing the campus of a European university, when he fell into conversation with a young man who was entering upon his studies in the field of law. "When you have completed your course," asked Philip, "what do you plan to do then?"

"Oh, I shall seek to gain a wide reputation," came the reply.

"And then?" inquired Philip.

"Why," said the student, "there is no doubt that I shall be promoted to a high office and grow rich."

"And then?" continued Philip.

"And then I shall live comfortably in honor and wealth and dignity," he replied.

"And then?" persisted Philip.

"And then . . . and then," stammered the boy, "I suppose I shall die."

Then Philip raised his voice and asked, "And what then?" The boy made no reply, but walked away rather ashamed and confused.

Most of you remember the name of Studdert Kennedy, that beloved English chaplain who made so deep an impression on all our boys during the first World War. Once he said that when he would finally appear before his Creator, he expected that God would ask him, "Well, what have you made of your life?"

Do not these instances point up in one way or other the deepest concern of our human nature—the desire for fulfillment? Usually it is not a problem relating to resources or to what we have, but to how we use our powers to become what we ought and to realize our potential in what we consider to be our highest purpose. Some among us think mistakenly that it is highly commendable merely to cherish an ideal, and that it is quite unimportant how we try to attain or realize it. But in the area of moral living it can never be a matter of the end justifying the means because always the means influences and indeed determines the character of the end. Jesus, on the eve of Calvary and in his great prayer in behalf of his disciples and their mission for the Kingdom, said, "For their sakes I consecrate myself that they also might be consecrated by the truth." Here he named the means that were commensurate in quality and vitality with the ends. Also he knew that in these ends alone his followers were to discover their highest fulfillment. What is more, each disciple had in his own way the same set of circumstances: an open destiny bracketed by two highly determinative words "I" and "myself." Jesus put the word "consecrate" in between them, but whenever through the ages his followers chose a lesser or weaker word, the future of his movement, of his Gospel, indeed of the Church itself, has been placed in real jeopardy.

There is one group with which you and I sometimes unconsciously identify ourselves and with whose members the word "congratulate" is their easiest choice. "I congratulate myself" is the slogan that runs through all their thinking and living. They have accepted without any question or even the slightest reflection the assurance of Henley's *Invictus:*

> I am the master of my fate:
> I am the captain of my soul.

Caught in the tide or mood of the times each makes himself the end, and the means is self too. As W. H. Elliott described it, "You are out for yourself, if you can and when you can."²⁵ And what makes the situation so distressing and the peril so real is that men and women hasten to congratulate themselves whenever their short-sighted philosophy pays off. "God helps those who help themselves," they cry. And with a pat on the back they shout, "It works!" They are like the little fellow who was asked if he said his prayers in the morning. "Of course not," he said, "I say my prayers at night because when I'm asleep I can't do anything. But when I'm awake I can look after myself."

But haven't you and I seen the inevitable result? The end, whatever it may have been, is not achieved, nor is it ever clearly seen, because, as Nikolai Berdyaev said, "Every attempt at looking at oneself is attended by the dangers of partiality, prejudice, vanity, and pretension."[26] This is why ours is such an unhappy generation. Most of us have so concentrated upon ourselves that inwardly there rages a civil war among our instincts and powers, and therefore few of us have ever known the blessings of peace of soul. What a long sea mile our intentions are from the costly word of Jesus, "I consecrate myself!" And how different are the ends! "I congratulate myself" may be flaunted in those moments of apparent triumph, but away down deep these are colossal blunders because in them you and I never face our inner selves or have a real or saving encounter with destiny.

Then there is a second group whose watchword is "I excuse myself." They may be compared with the lad named Jimmie who fell asleep habitually during his English classes much to the annoyance of the instructor. Finally one day the teacher in a fit of impatience shouted, "Jimmie, who wrote Hamlet?" And poor Jimmie, wakened suddenly from his napping, blurted out, "P-p-lease, ma'am, it wasn't me!"

And this is indicative of the way some people try to get through life today. It is never "me." It is always somebody else or something else. If it is not the church, it is the government, or some other institution. But regardless of who or what it is, this strategy, "I excuse myself," has invariably a double result: a growing attitude of indifference on the part of those who excuse themselves with such bad grace and a mood of sullen reproach on the part of those who have been burdened with more than their share of responsibility. And in no place has this creed produced more harmful results than in the organizations of the Christian Church. Never have more people been engaged in such a multiplicity of activities in the church as there are today, and certainly our statistics continue to be impressive. But have you ever examined these carefully in order to ascertain whether or not these busy people are actually facing up to the serious issues of the Kingdom of God or merely using their busy-ness to camouflage an attitude of sheer irresponsibility? Whenever any one of us lives in this way, he soon loses sight of those higher spiritual objectives without which no one of us can save himself from failure in any moral emergency.

I congratulate myself! I excuse myself! These philosophies are in the saddle today, and they are driving us. As long as self is the means and self the end, we are doomed never to be more than what our own selves can create or outline. But, says Abraham Heschel, "to worship God is to forget self."[27] In God's House a shift occurs in our focus and our self-consciousness is replaced by self-surrender. We no longer congratulate or excuse ourselves because, in the presence of God, the self is eclipsed and God becomes not something to be used, but someone to be adored and served. To worship means to bring God back into the structure of your world and mine. Jesus' whole life was constituted in this way, and in comparison with his record of faith and devotion, all our self-reliance appears poor and shabby. "I consecrate myself" was his high resolve even when the clouds of hate and revenge were lowering upon his path. No one could accuse him of putting self in the central arena of things. And the words he used reflected the integrity of his soul and made clear to every rising generation the nature and quality of this new life he would have us all appropriate and support.

The consecrated life is, first of all, a *concerned* life. Jesus said, "For their sakes. . . ." He had a serious concern for men, which differed so radically from the other religious leaders and thinkers of his time, particularly the Stoics. Now the Stoics aimed at creating a desert in the human heart so that an attitude of "I don't care" would color their reactions to every case of human need and helplessness. One of the chief words in the Stoic's vocabulary was ἀπάθεια, from which comes our English word *apathy,* and for him it meant a state of life in which the flame of sympathy had flickered out and had been replaced by a grim sense of self-reliance and self-control. "Their aim," writes William Barclay, "was to banish sympathy from life."

But Jesus said, "For their sakes. . . ." And here he disclosed the greatest spiritual principle by which any one of us can ever live. It is the principle by which you invest all that you have and are and can ever be into the moral well-being of others and into the realization through them of God's sacred cause. Moreover, this principle cuts straight across the way of life of all the twentieth century Stoics whom we meet every day: the people in whose lives the springs of love and pity have become dried up and a ruthless individualism suppresses any concern they might have for the plea of others. Indeed no man among us can ever reach the highest fulfillment of God's will for his life until all the ambitions and ideals of his inner nature are baptized into the name of Christ and under the aegis of his spirit are used in devotion to the needs of men. Robert Southwell once said, "Not where I breathe, but where I love, I live." And love is the partner of consecration, for when a man truly loves, he truly cares, and the outgoings of his life are for somebody's sake. "For their sakes" then is more than merely an index of good intentions or the mark of philanthropy in community life. Within the reality of Christian worship it becomes a voice that shifts you and me from narrow and unrelenting preoccupation with ourselves to a vital concern for others that God's best purposes be realized fully in them.

On further thought, the consecrated life is a *controlled* life. There was more to what Jesus said. "For their sakes I consecrate myself" would seem to be all that anyone could ask or dare to expect; but Jesus took care to make assurance doubly sure and specified that only through the truth could this richer life of service be brought to maturity. Originally "to consecrate" meant "to set apart" for divine use. And here Jesus named *truth* as the all-embracing agent which should claim his followers once they were chosen. And in this case the truth was the Good News that into a world of sin and of dying hopes, God had sent his Son to save and redeem it. Truth was alive once and for all in a Person and its nature and essence was love. As Paul declared, "God was in Christ reconciling the world unto himself" (2 Cor. 5:19). Moreover, Jesus' followers were then and are now to find the meaning and fulfillment of life in and through that Gospel. Once they were set apart, this Gospel would take control of their lives but deliberately for the sake of God's other creatures.

This, however, is not abstract theory; it is history. One day a young Oxford don chose Christ, and eventually, through the consecration of John Wesley, the whole course and current of English history were changed. On another day a young Boston shoe salesman chose Christ and thereupon, through the consecration of Dwight L. Moody, the North American continent began to throb from the spiritual contagion of his flaming evangelism. On still another day a young factory worker in Blantyre, Scotland, chose Christ and soon, through the consecration of David Livingstone, the heart of Africa became sensitive to the higher levels of moral living. In every case theirs was a concerned life, but the secret of it was that they were claimed by a Gospel; they were under its control; their prayer was Jeremy Taylor's plea: "Let my body be servant of my spirit and both my body and my spirit servants of Jesus Christ."

In view of what we have said, the consecrated life has to be basically a *committed* life. When any man's life is fully consecrated, he has a new concern; he is under a new control; but the ultimate efficacy of it all depends upon the depth and vitality of his personal commitment to Jesus Christ.

James S. Stewart[28] tells of a young man who went out from the town of Devon, England, to become a shipman in the fleet of Sir Francis Drake. Once during a visit back home he met an old schoolmate who had remained ashore and had become fat and lazy upon the land and who turned to the sailor and remarked with a smirk of derision, "Well, you haven't made much out of all these years, have you?" "No," said the shipman, "I guess I haven't. I've been cold, hungry, and shipwrecked, and often I've been dreadfully frightened, but I've been with the greatest Captain who ever sailed the seas."

Consecration! Yes, it can be for every one of us a glorious adventure, but at its highest and best it demands a personal commitment which can be the costliest business in all the world. Yet in every age it has been just this decisive commitment to the person of Jesus Christ which has liberated men and women from the flabby worship of self and has sent them across seas, into jungles, and over mountain crags with their banners emblazoned with the words, "For their sakes I consecrate myself." Each of these, moreover, would testify with candor that this commitment was no mere "off the cuff" decision or a choice among several equally good or respectable jobs; but that on one occasion in the worship of the Church the plan of God and the need of man came together into blazing focus and for that tremendous moment they saw in clearest lines the work of Christ in the redemption of the human race and the glorious fulfillment when everything would be gathered up and consummated in him.

Speaking of St. Paul and his commitment, Dr. Stewart puts it into his own stirring lines:

The great frowning mountain ranges of Asia were no barrier to this man, for beyond them men were dying without Christ. Down to the shores of the Aegean Sea he came, and in the wind across the Western seas he heard dimly the cry of myriads without hope and without God in their world. Always as he turned his gaze toward Corinth, Rome, and Spain, the Christ in his heart was yearn-ing with a great compassion for those sheep who were without a shepherd. Always there was a driving sense of an unseen compulsion, 'Necessity is laid upon me: woe is me, if I preach not the Gospel!'[29]

This was one man's commitment. And although it carried him to stoning, shipwreck, imprisonment, and finally to death, yet he maintained stoutly and vigorously, "I count all things but loss for the excellence of the knowledge of Christ Jesus my Lord: for whom I have suffered the loss of all things, and do count them but refuse, that I may win Christ, and be found in him. . . ." (Philipp. 3:8, 9).

How ordinary and tawdry do your efforts and mine appear in the face of such unqualified consecration! How trivial can be our life's story as we strut along in the regalia of our own vanity or as we raise defences behind which to excuse ourselves! But what a difference is made when in the act of worship we are brought face to face with the facts of our own life and the Fact of Christ! Andrew Bonar once said, "I see that when I dwell at any length of time upon myself, my heart is not profited; but whenever I get a sight of Christ's love, my heart is full of life."[30] This is the story that is repeated again and again as men and women see the character of the living Christ unveiled in the proclamation of the Church and his love made real in the symbols of his broken body and shed blood. Life's pattern is renewed. Life's purpose is restored. And with a new commitment to Christ and the cause of humanity, they toil and pray until the job is done. Then one day they will stand upon the rim of the years and looking back upon life's story will shout with a radiant sense of victory, "I may have lost everything in life's voyage, but I have been with the greatest Captain that ever sailed the seas!"

Notes

Chapter One

1. H. H. Farmer, *The Servant of the Word*, p. *v*. Nisbet & Co., Ltd., 1941.
2. P. T. Forsyth, *Positive Preaching and the Modern Mind*, p. 106. A. C. Armstrong & Son, 1907.
3. Edwin C. Dargan, *A History of Preaching*, p. 9. Baker Book House, 1954.
4. Gerald C. Matthews, *The Craftsmanship of the Preacher*, p. 1. Faith Press, 1955.
5. Douglas Webster, *What Is Evangelism?* p. 113. Highway Press, 1959.
6. W. B. J. Martin, *Five Minutes to Twelve*, p. 108. Collins, 1957.
7. Helen Gardner, *The Art of T. S. Eliot*, p. 68. Cresset Press, 1949.
8. Forsyth, *op. cit.*, p. 97.
9. Raymond Abba, *Principles of Christian Worship*, p. 5. Oxford University Press, 1957.
10. John Calvin, *Tracts:* "The Necessity of Reforming the Church" (trans. Henry Beveridge), p. 247. The Calvin Translation Society, 1844.
11. Frank Colquhoun (ed.) *The Living Church: A Symposium*, p. 25. Church Book Room Press, 1952.
12. George D. Henderson, *Transactions of the Scottish Ecclesiological Society*, XII, ii, p. 66.
13. Forsyth, *The Church and the Sacraments*, p. 134. Independent Press, 1917.
14. Forsyth, *Positive Preaching and the Modern Mind*, p. 98.

Chapter Two

1. Frederick W. Schroeder, *Preaching the Word with Authority*, p. 8. Westminster Press, 1954.
2. R. E. C. Browne, *The Ministry of the Word*, p. 73. Student Christian Movement Press, 1958.
3. J. H. Jowett, *The Preacher, His Life and Work*, p. 141. Hodder and Stoughton, 1912.
4. A. J. Gossip, *The Galilean Accent*, p. 11. T. & T. Clark, 1927.
5. Gossip, *From the Edge of the Crowd*, pp. 227, 228. T. & T. Clark, 1926.
6. Gossip, *The Hero in Thy Soul*, pp. 86, 87. Charles Scribner's Sons.
7. Browne, *op. cit.*, p. 19.
8. Frederick B. Speakman, *The Salty Tang*, p. 48. Fleming H. Revell, 1954.
9. *Ibid.*, pp. 69, 70.
10. *Ibid.*, p. 146.
11. H. H. Farmer, "The Preacher and Persons," *Review and Expositor*, Vol. XLIII, p. 411.
12. J. C. Shairp, "Prose Poets: Cardinal Newman," *Aspects of Poetry*, p. 444. Oxford University Press, 1881.

13. H. E. Fosdick, *The Living of These Days,* pp. 94f. Harper & Brothers, 1956.

14. Joseph Dawson, *The Soul of the Sermon,* p. 68. Simpkin, Marshall & Co., 1895.

15. Farmer, *The Servant of the Word,* p. 64.

16. Randolph Quirk, "Colloquial English in Communication," *Studies in Communication,* ed. by B. Ifor Evans, p. 180. Secker & Warburg, 1955.

17. Edward R. Murrow, "The Responsibilities of Television," *The Press and the People,* Nos. 8 & 9, p. 4 (Fund for the Republic).

18. Quoted by John A. Broadus, *On the Preparation and Delivery of Sermons* (Revised edition), p. 223. Harper & Brothers, 1944.

19. Ezra Pound, letters quoted by Herbert Read, *The True Voice of Feeling,* p. 126. Faber & Faber, 1953.

20. Quoted by Gilbert Monk in *The Young Preacher's Guide,* p. 436. E. Stock, 1905.

21. Quoted by A. Philip in *Thoughts on Worship and Preaching,* p. 64. James Clarke, 1931.

22. William Cowper, "Preachers: The True vs. the Insincere," *Masterpieces of Religious Verse,* ed. by J. D. Morrison, p. 498. Harper & Brothers, 1948.

Chapter Three

1. William M. Taylor, *The Ministry of the Word,* p. 29. A. D. F. Randolph, 1876.

2. Karl Barth, *The Word of God and the Word of Man,* p. 100. Harper & Brothers, 1957.

3. R. H. Fuller, "The Word of God," *Theology,* Vol. XLVII, p. 271.

4. F. D. Coggan, *The Ministry of the Word,* p. 14. Canterbury Press, 1945.

5. Quoted by Coggan, *ibid.,* p. 80.

6. James S. Stewart, *A Faith to Proclaim,* pp. 14, 15. Charles Scribner's Sons, 1953.

7. F. W. Dillistone, *Christianity and Communication,* p. 125. Charles Scribner's Sons, 1956.

8. Quoted by G. H. S. Walpole, *The Greatest Service in the World,* pp. 118, 119. Wells, Gardner, Darton & Co., 1924.

9. Barth, *op. cit.,* pp. 49, 50.

10. Leslie Tizard, *Preaching: The Art of Communication,* p. 18. George Allen & Unwin, Ltd., 1958.

11. Phillips Brooks, *Eight Lectures on Preaching,* p. 8. S.P.C.K., 1959.

12. H. A. Hodges, *Wilhelm Dilthey: An Introduction,* pp. 25–35. Oxford University Press, 1944.

13. A. F. Kirkpatrick, *The Psalms,* p. 431. Cambridge University Press, 1957.

14. Samuel Terrien, *The Psalms and Their Meaning for Today,* p. 256. Bobbs-Merrill, 1952.

15. Kyle M. Yates, *Preaching from the Psalms,* p. 25. Harper & Brothers, 1948.

16. Sheldon H. Blank, "Nearness of God and Psalm 73," *To Do and Teach,* p. 2. College of the Bible, 1953.

17. Norman Snaith, *Hymns of the Temple,* p. 106. SCM Press, 1951.

18. George Johnstone Jeffery (ed.), *The Sacramental Table,* p. 84. Harper & Brothers, 1952.

19. See *Interpretation,* Vol. XII, p. 421.

Chapter Four

1. F. Spitta, *Zur Geschichte und Litteratur des Urchristentums*, I, p. 289. Vandenhoeck und Ruprecht, 1893.
2. Hugh T. Kerr, "The Story of the Book of Common Worship," *Journal of the Presbyterian Historical Society*, Vol. XXIX, No. 4, p. 196.
3. C. W. Dugmore, *The Influence of the Synagogue upon the Divine Office*, p. 2. Oxford University Press, 1944.
4. L. Duchesne, *Christian Worship*, (trans. M. L. McLure), p. 46. S.P.C.K., 1903.
5. A. B. McDonald, *Christian Worship in the Primitive Church*, p. 60. T. & T. Clark, 1934.
6. Oscar Cullmann, *Essays on the Lord's Supper*, p. 16. John Knox Press, 1958.
7. James Denney, *The Death of Christ*, p. 46. Hodder & Stoughton, 1903.
8. *Cf.* J. Klausner, *Jesus of Nazareth;* A. J. B. Higgins: *The Lord's Supper in the New Testament;* J. Jeremias: *The Eucharistic Words of Jesus.*
9. J. H. Srawley, *The Early History of the Liturgy* (2nd Edition), pp. 2, 3. Cambridge University Press, 1947.
10. W. D. Maxwell, *An Outline of Christian Worship*, pp. 5, 6. Oxford University Press, 1936.
11. Neville Clark, *An Approach to the Theology of the Sacraments*, p. 44. S.C.M. Press, 1956.
12. T. W. Manson, "The Jewish Background," in *Christian Worship*, p. 46, ed. by N. Micklem. Oxford University Press, 1936.
13. William Sanday, *Outlines of Life of Christ*, p. 162. Charles Scribner's Sons, 1905.
14. G. H. C. MacGregor, *Eucharistic Origins*, p. 23. James Clarke, 1928.
15. MacDonald, *op. cit.*, pp. 140–153. Cullmann, *op. cit.*, pp. 17–23.
16. J. W. Hunkin, "The Origin of Eucharistic Doctrine," *The Evangelical Doctrine of Holy Communion*, p. 14, ed. by A. J. MacDonald. W. Heffer & Sons, 1930.
17. Cullmann, *op. cit.*, p. 19.
18. Forsyth, *The Church and the Sacraments*, pp. 220, 221.
19. *Ibid.*, pp. 215, 216.
20. Eusebius, *Ecclesiastical History* (trans. Lawlor and Oulton), Vol. IV, v, p. 106. S.P.C.K., 1927.
21. Dugmore, *op. cit.*, p. 5.
22. H. Leitzmann, "The Christian Church in the West," *Cambridge Ancient History*, Vol. XII, pp. 523, 524.
23. MacDonald, *op. cit.*, p. 4.
24. See *Apostolic Fathers* (ed. by Lightfoot), Vol. II, 1, pp. 13–21. Macmillan Company, 1885.
25. B. H. Streeter, *The Primitive Church*, pp. 279–287. Macmillan Company, 1929.
26. From *Early Christian Fathers*. Published 1953. The Westminster Press. Used by permission.
27. *First Apology of Justin Martyr*, Ante-Nicene Christian Library, Vol. II, Chaps. LXV-LXVII, pp. 63–65 (Roberts and Donaldson). T. & T. Clark, 1867.
28. Irenaeus, *Against Heresies, ibid.*, IV, 18:4–6.
29. *The Epistles of Cyprian*, Chap. LXII, 14, *ibid.*, Vol. VIII, p. 218.
30. Tertullian, *Against Marcion*, Chap. IV, 40, *ibid.*, Vol. VII, pp. 351–354.

31. D. H. Hislop, *Our Heritage in Christian Worship*, p. 85. T. &. T. Clark, 1936.
32. A. Harnack, *Outlines of the History of Dogma* (trans. E. K. Mitchell), p. 112. Funk & Wagnalls Co., 1893.
33. R. M. Adamson, *The Christian Doctrine of the Lord's Supper*, p. 38. T. & T. Clark, 1905.
34. *Ibid.*, p. 39.
35. Thomas Leishmann, *The Moulding of the Scottish Reformation*, p. 6. Lee Lecture, 1897. Wm. Blackwood, 1897.
36. *The Book of Ratramnus on The Body and Blood of the Lord* (Trans. J. Taylor), c, ci. Lord, 1855.
37. James Moffatt, "Luther," in Micklem, *op. cit.*, p. 120.
38. *Ibid.*, p. 125.
39. *Ibid.*, p. 136.
40. Maxwell, *op. cit.*, p. 74.
41. M. Luther, *Opera Latina* (Frankfort Edition), V, 35, p. 317. Wace & Buchkeim, 1865.
42. H. Zwingli, *Opera*, III, pp. 605, 606. Zurich, 1832.
43. *Ibid.*, ii, p. 212.
44. J. S. Whale, "Calvin," in Micklem, *op. cit.*, p. 167.
45. Hislop, *op. cit.*, p. 184.
46. C. J. Cadoux, "Zwingli," in Micklem, *op. cit.*, p. 153.
47. C. W. Baird, *Presbyterian Liturgies*, p. 14. Baker Book House, 1957.
48. C. H. Smyth, *Cranmer and the Reformation under Edward VI*, p. 155. Cambridge University Press, 1926.
49. Maxwell, *op. cit.*, p. 111.
50. Whale, *op. cit.*, p. 171.
51. R. D. Richardson, "Christian Worship in the New Reformation," *Modern Churchman*, Vol. XL, p. 300.
52. Calvin, *op. cit.*, I, p. 139.
53. T. H. L. Parker, *Oracles of God*, p. 139. Lutterworth, 1947.
54. E. Doumergue, *Jean Calvin*, II, p. 504. Bridel, 1902.
55. A. M. Fairbairn, "Worship," *Studies in Religion and Theology*, p. 264. Hodder & Stoughton, 1910.
56. Wm. Cunningham, *The Reformers and the Theology of the Reformation*, p. 4. T. & T. Clark, 1862.
57. Herman Bavinck, "Calvin and Common Grace," *Princeton Theological Review*, Vol. VII, 1909, p. 463.
58. Adolf Deissmann, *St. Paul* (trans. L. R. M. Strachan), p. 130. Hodder & Stoughton, 1912.
59. A. Barclay, *The Protestant Doctrine of the Lord's Supper*, p. 121. Jackson, Wylie, 1927.
60. Forsyth, *op. cit.*, p. 121.
61. Baird, *op. cit.*, p. 194.
62. D. Bruce Nicol, "The Church Service Society—A Brief Retrospect," *CSS Annual*, 1928–29, p. 19.
63. From *The Book of Common Worship*. Copyright 1946 by the Presbyterian Board of Christian Education. Used by permission.
64. F. W. Powicke, *The Reformation in England*, p. 1. Oxford University Press, 1941.
65. C. A. Briggs, "The Principles of Puritanism," *The Presbyterian Review*, V, 1884, p. 665.

66. Horton Davies, *The Worship of English Puritans*, p. 3. Dacre Press, Westminster Press, 1948.

67. Einar Molland, *Christendom*, p. 279. Philosophical Library, 1959.

68. Davies, *Christian Worship*, p. 68. Abingdon Press, 1957.

69. C. H. Heimsath, *The Genius of Public Worship*, p. 100. Charles Scribner's Sons, 1947.

70. Nolan B. Harmon, *The Rites and Ritual of Episcopal Methodism*, pp. 48, 49. Publishing House of Methodist Episcopal Church South, 1926.

71. P. Edwall, E. Hayman, & W. D. Maxwell, *Ways of Worship*, p. 160. Harper & Brothers, 1951.

72. B. Manning, *Essays in Orthodox Dissent*, p. 56. Independent Press, 1939.

Chapter Five

1. J. D. Benoît, *Liturgical Renewal:* Studies in Catholic and Protestant Developments on the Continent, p. 59. SCM Press, 1958.

2. Howard Hageman, "The Liturgical Revival," *Theology Today*, Vol. VII, p. 494.

3. *Edinburgh Review*, Vol. XCV, No. CXCIV, p. 455.

4. George F. MacLeod, *One Way Left*, p. 98. Iona, 1956.

5. Whale, *op. cit.*, p. 165.

6. *God's Will in Our Time*, General Assembly of the Church of Scotland. SCM Press, 1942.

7. Farmer, *The Servant of the Word*, pp. 18, 19.

8. *Ibid.*, p. 23.

9. Humbert de Romans, *Treatise on Preaching*, pp. 6, 7, ed. by W. M. Conlon. Blackfriars, 1955.

10. Farmer, *op. cit.*, pp. 11, 12.

11. A. A. Cowan, *The Primacy of Preaching*, p. 13. T. & T. Clark, 1955.

12. John Bishop, *Study Notes on Preaching and Worship*, p. 52. Epworth Press, 1949.

13. Daniel Jenkins, *The Strangeness of the Church*, p. 82. Doubleday & Co., 1955.

14. Henderson, *Church and Ministry*, p. 42. Baird Lecture, 1950. Hodder & Stoughton, 1951.

15. Robert S. Simpson, *Ideas in Corporate Worship*, p. 17. T. & T. Clark, 1927.

16. Forsyth, *Positive Preaching and the Modern Mind*, p. 51.

17. E. R. Micklem, *Our Approach to God*, p. 19. Hodder & Stoughton, 1934.

18. From the *Book of Common Order of the Church of Scotland*. By permission of the Church of Scotland Committee on Public Worship and Aids to Devotion.

19. *Loc. cit.*, pp. 30, 31.

20. Oswald B. Milligan, *The Ministry of the Word*, p. 29. Oxford University Press, 1941.

21. Gerhard Tersteegen, "Lo, God is here!" (trans. John Wesley,) *The Hymnary*, p. 18. The United Church Publishing House, 1930.

22. Simpson, *op. cit.*, p. 60.

23. A. A. Mackenzie, *Transactions of the Scottish Ecclesiological Society*, Vol. XII, *iii*, p. 107.

24. Bishop, *op. cit.*, p. 7.

25. Robert Bruce, *The Mystery of the Lord's Supper*, ed. by Thos. F. Torrance, pp. 84, 85. James Clarke, 1958.

26. Harold Roberts, "Fellowship in Worship," *The Expository Times*, Vol. XLIX, pp. 214ff.
27. D. H. Hislop, "The Basis of Worship," *ibid.*, pp. 149ff.
28. Simpson, *op. cit.*, p. 81.
29. David G. Peck, *Living Worship*, p. 39. Eyre & Spottiswoode, 1944.
30. John Calvin, *Institutes of the Christian Religion*, Bk. IV, ch xvii, 39, p. 596. Wm. B. Eerdman's, 1953.

Chapter Six

1. See Baird, *op. cit.*, p. 22 (footnote).
2. Augustine, *Confessions*, VII, 17. Basic Writings of Saint Augustine, Vol. I, p. 104. Random House, 1948.
3. Robert Will, *Le Culte*, Vol. I, p. 318. Libraire Istra, Maison d'Edition de l'Imprimerie Strasbourgeoise, 1925.
4. A. G. Reynolds, "The Church: Its Worship," *The Living Church*, ed. by H. W. Vaughan, p. 100. The United Church Publishing House, 1949.
5. *The Book of Common Order* of the United Church of Canada (1950 edition), p. 2.
6. W. D. Maxwell, "The Sunday Morning Service," CSS *Annual*, 1930–31, p. 32.
7. J. H. S. Burleigh, "The Reformed Tradition in Christian Worship," *ibid.*, 1959, p. 8.
8. Maxwell, *op. cit.*, 1929–30, p. 25.

Chapter Seven

1. Jemima Luke, "I think when I read . . . ," *The Hymnbook*, p. 386. John Ribble, 1955.
2. *Macbeth*, III, iv, line 24.
3. Evelyn Underhill, "Light of Christ," *The Fruits of the Spirit*, p. 89. Longmans, Green and Co., 1956.
4. H. E. Fosdick, *The Three Meanings*, III, p. 15. Association Press, 1950.
5. Albert Schweitzer, quoted by John Baillie in *A Diary of Readings*, p. 45. Charles Scribner's Sons, 1955.
6. William Law, *Serious Call to a Devout and Holy Life*, p. 231. J. M. Dent, 1905.
7. K. Heim, "The Law of Sacrifice," *The Expository Times*, Vol. XLVII, p. 559.
8. Yates, *op. cit.*, p. 139.
9. Lesslie Newbigin, *Sin and Salvation*, p. 14. SCM Book Club, 1956.
10. Webster, *op. cit.*, p. 46.
11. W. Robertson Nicoll, *Ian MacLaren*, p. 26. Dodd, Mead & Co., 1908.
12. Frederick R. Meek, *The Life to Live*, pp. 22f. Oxford University Press, 1955.
13. *The Book of Common Worship*, p. 169.
14. Horatius Bonar, "Here, O my Lord," *The Hymnbook*, p. 372.
15. Venantius Fortunatus, "Welcome, happy morning!" (trans. by John Ellerton). *The Hymnbook*, p. 186.
16. Emil Brunner, *The Great Invitation*, p. 64. Westminster Press, 1955.
17. H. F. Lovell Cocks, "The Communion of the Holy Spirit," *The Expository Times*, Vol. LXVIII, p. 250.
18. James A. Pike, *Beyond Anxiety*, p. 145. Charles Scribner's Sons, 1954.

19. Quoted by H. E. Fosdick, *op. cit.*, p. 11.
20. Quoted by John Ferguson in *Christian Faith for Today*, p. 68. Source Publishers, 1956.
21. Ferguson, *op. cit.*, p. 72.
22. Fosdick, *What Is Vital in Religion*, p. 135. Harper & Brothers, 1955.
23. Quoted by Vincent Ross in "The Truth that Ends Our Falseness," *The Expository Times*, Vol. LXI, p. 213.
24. Ian MacPherson, *None Other Name*, p. 22. Epworth Press, 1946.
25. W. H. Elliott, *Man to Man*, p. 41. Skeffington & Son, Ltd., 1944.
26. Nikolai Berdyaev, *Dream and Reality*, quoted by T. Tudor Rhys in *The Expository Times*, Vol. LXIII, p. 133.
27. Abraham Heschel, "Prayer and Theological Discipline," *Union Seminary Quarterly Review*, Vol. XIV, No. 4. p. 4.
28. James S. Stewart, *op. cit.*, p. 151.
29. *Ibid.*, p. 155.
30. Quoted by Robert Prenter in *The Religion of a Common Man*, p. 21. James Clarke, 1947.

Index of Proper Names

A

Abba, Raymond, 13
Adamson, R. M., 60, 61
Ainsworth, H., 84
Aquinas, Thos., 61
Asbury, Francis, 128

B

Bancroft, Richard, 81
Barclay, Wm., 148, 161
Barnes, E. W., 53
Barth, K., 29, 32
Bavinck, H., 69
Baxter, R., 79, 80
Beethoven, L. von, 148
Benoit, J. D., 93
Berdyaev, N., 159
Bishop, John, 101, 112
Bonar, Andrew, 164
Brilioth, Y., 53
Brooks, P., 33, 153
Bruce, Robt., 113
Bucer, M., 65, 68, 71, 78
Buchanan, James, 27
Buffon, Geo. L., 25
Bunyan, John, 80
Burleigh, J. H. S., 126
Buttrick, Geo. A., 21
Browne, R. E. C., 19
Brunner, E., 100, 152

C

Calvin, J., 14, 62, 65–71, 72, 77–80,
96, 97, 110, 115, 118, 123

Carey, Wm., 86
Carmen, Bliss, 155
Cartwright, Thos., 79–81
Chalmers, Thos., 24, 27
Charles I, 73
Chrysostom, 15
Clark, Neville, 48
Clark, H. W., 82
Cocks, H. F. L., 152, 155
Coverdale, Miles, 78
Cowper, Wm., 27
Cranmer, Thos., 70, 78
Cromwell, Oliver, 74
Cullmann, Oscar, 51, 52
Cyprian, 59, 60

D

Dale, R. W., 84
Dargan, E. C., 8
Davidson, R., 29
Davies, Horton, 81, 82, 85
Dawson, Joseph, 23
Deissmann, A., 69
Denney, James, 24, 48
Dilthy, Wilhelm, 34
Doddridge, P., 84
Doumergue, E., 61, 68, 128
Drummond, H., 144
Duchesne, L. M., 47
Dugmore, C. W., 54

E

Edward VI, 78
Eliot, T. S., 12
Elliott, W. H., 158
Erasmus, 62, 64
Eusebius, 54

173

264.057
M16